DR. ART ULENE'S

Luscious, Low-Fat

Desserts

RECIPES BY MARY WARD

Health
POINTS ™
1996

This book has been written and published strictly for informational purposes, and in no way should it be used as a substitute for consultation with your medical doctor or health care professional. The author and publisher are providing the information in this book so that you can have the knowledge and can choose, at your own risk, to act on that knowledge. The author and publisher urge all readers to be aware of their health status and to consult health professionals before beginning any health or fitness program, including changes in dietary habits.

Nutritional values for the recipes in this book have been computed using Nutritionist III™, Version 7.2, First DataBank (formerly N-Squared Computing), San Bruno, California.

Published by HealthPOINTS,
16601 Ventura Blvd., Encino, CA 91436

ISBN: 0-932513-09-03

Printed in USA by RR Donnelley & Sons Co.

10 9 8 7 6 5 4 3 2

DR. ART ULENE'S

Luscious, Low-Fat

Desserts

RECIPES BY MARY WARD

Quick & Easy

As a special feature in LUSCIOUS, LOW-FAT DESSERTS, quick and easy recipes are indicated throughout the book with the ◐ symbol. These recipes require minimal preparation and cooking time, generally under thirty minutes. They are also listed in the index under the heading *Quick & Easy*.

Illustrations by Aly Walsh and Mark Alhadeff.

Photos by PhotoDisc™ Images © 1996 PhotoDisc, Inc.: cover and pages 11, 13, 15, 19, 20, 53, 57, 77, 81, 83, 90, 145, 146, 147, 148, 149, 150, 151, & 154.

Contents

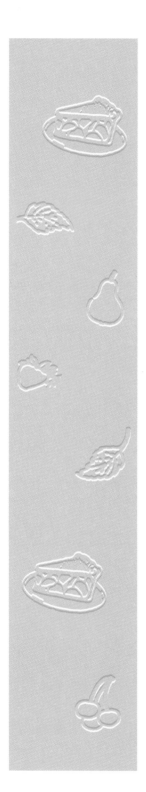

Cover Photo: Lemon Meringue Pie, see page 54 for recipe.

INTRODUCTION

To some people, it may seem hard to believe that a physician who is committed to promoting good nutrition would create a cookbook filled with recipes for desserts. But this book will not surprise people who are familiar with my philosophy about food or with my educational efforts. This book is just another tool to be used for promoting health while enjoying life to its fullest.

We eat food because we must. Food is the fuel that powers every bodily process. It provides the vitamins essential for normal function and the minerals necessary for normal structure.

But food gives us much more. It is the source of enormous sensory pleasure. It is the focal point of many critical family interactions and it is the centerpiece of many important customs and celebrations.

Food has also been blamed for causing some serious health problems, such as obesity, high blood pressure, coronary heart disease and cancer. But food is not the culprit; poor choices of food are at fault. So, to enjoy good health, it is not necessary to give up desserts and all the other foods you like—as some have suggested. Rather, you just need to make wiser choices in these important categories.

Did I say important categories? Desserts—important? Yes, because they contribute much to our enjoyment of life, and because they contribute significantly to the quality of our nutrition when they are well-chosen. This book will help you make such choices.

In the pages that follow, you will find a wide variety of delicious desserts created by my long-time friend and collaborator, Mary Ward. Her recipes are low in fat (no recipe gets more that 20 percent of its calories from fat,) but high in important nutrients—and very high in taste. But you don't have to limit your dessert choices to Mary's recipes. In Chapter 1, we'll show you how to modify your own favorite recipes so they are lower in fat and better for your health but still great fun to eat. With a little guidance, you *can* have your cake and eat it, too.

So, enjoy yourself. Best wishes to you for good health always.

Arthur Ulene, MD

The Basics

A little *basic* know-how goes a long way when preparing low-fat sweets. In this chapter, learn how to enhance flavor and texture when using the recipes in this book... and when transforming your own recipes into luscious, low-fat favorites.

USING THE RECIPES IN THIS BOOK & ADAPTING YOUR OLD-TIME FAVORITES

As promised in the Introduction, you don't have to sacrifice good desserts to reduce the fat in your diet. Low-fat desserts are not only possible, but also delicious and easy to prepare. In this chapter, you'll find specific recommendations for maximizing the results of the recipes in this book and for transforming some of your favorite high-fat recipes into low-fat alternatives.

With some thoughtful substitutions, you can continue to use your favorite dessert recipes while following a low-fat eating plan. Some of the alterations are obvious, such as substituting nonfat milk for whole milk and nonfat sour cream or yogurt for regular sour cream. Other substitutions may not be as evident, but they are just as simple to make. In most cases, you will still retain the flavor of the original recipes using these savvy substitutions.

Substitutions do not, however, tell the whole story in low-fat desserts. Certain equipment and specific ingredients also enhance both adapted recipes and those in this book. Remember, low-fat desserts involve the cutting back of fat; to do this and still maintain a supple texture and a delicious taste, you must follow some basic guidelines.

EQUIPMENT

To get the most from the recipes in this book, you will need a sifter, a blender, a food processor and an electric mixer. Here's why:

Sifter: In some traditional recipes, you can skip sifting the dry ingredients, resulting in little difference to the end product. However, in a low-fat dessert, especially baked desserts, sifting is a very important step in achieving a light and airy consistency. So, please do not skip this step; follow it as a mandatory part of the recipe.

Blender: This is an especially useful tool in the frozen desserts section and in the children's chapter. In most other places where a blender is used, you can substitute a food processor.

Food Processor: Working with fruit purées makes it imperative to have a food processor available. It is also very helpful in making crusts. However, when buying a food processor, don't be fooled by the expensive models with multiple attachments. An inexpensive one will work fine for most of your needs.

Electric Mixer: While you can use an old-fashioned hand beater, an electric mixer makes it much easier to create cakes, meringues and other favorite desserts. In these recipes, beating ingredients is very important as it helps compensate for the textural lightness normally provided by fat. So, when beating is called for, do not skimp on the duration or intensity.

HELPFUL, BUT NOT ABSOLUTELY NECESSARY, EQUIPMENT
Food Mill: This is an inexpensive, helpful addition to any kitchen. Operated by hand, it can be used to purée a small amount of fruit for a recipe, without all the extra cleanup of a food processor.

Ice Cream Maker: In Ices, Sorbets, Gelati & Toppings, some recipes use an ice cream maker. While this appliance will certainly make these recipes easier, full instructions are also provided for making them without an ice cream maker.

Glass Pans: When baking, we suggest using oven-safe glass pans. When we developed the recipes for this book, our testing showed that glass pans out-performed metal pans. In most cases, cakes baked in metal tend to shrink whereas those baked in glass hold their size. This shrinkage probably results because metal heats up very quickly as opposed to the slow-heating of glass. This shrinkage problem is especially true of the commonly used inexpensive aluminum pans. So, if available, use glass baking pans.

A note of caution—be careful using glassware when preparing frozen desserts as glass can crack in the freezer.

INGREDIENTS
Buying top-quality ingredients enhances any recipe. Low-fat sweets require that the other ingredients make up for the flavor that is lost when you cut out or

reduce fat. With this in mind, follow these guidelines when buying ingredients:

When a recipe calls for sugar, always buy pure cane sugar. This is granulated sugar and confectioners sugar cannot be substituted for it.

Vanilla extract is an important ingredient for flavor. While it is more expensive than imitation vanilla, it is worth every penny in flavor.

When using buttermilk in these recipes, use the lowest fat version available. In some areas, nonfat buttermilk is readily available and this will reduce the fat content in a recipe while still retaining the flavor. However, if nonfat buttermilk is unavailable, use 1% or 2% and you will still have a low-fat, delicious dessert. The nutritional values for the recipes in this book were calculated using 1% buttermilk.

In some of the recipes, buttermilk is used as a leavening agent when combined with baking soda. Allow this mixture to set for at least five minutes or until it gets slightly bubbly on the surface.

For recipes that call for cocoa, always use a European-style cocoa powder. This unsweetened cocoa is relatively low in fat and rich in flavor.

When substituting for whole eggs, we suggest egg whites (two per egg) instead of today's egg substitutes that can be bought at the market. Egg whites are cheaper, all natural and without fat. It is important in many recipes that whipped egg whites form stiff peaks. For the best results, whip egg whites in a clean, warm, copper or glass bowl.

SUBSTITUTIONS
The simplest way to reduce the amount of fat in your favorite desserts is to substitute reduced-fat products, fruit purées and some intense liquid sweeteners (molasses, honey) for the traditional high-fat ingredients. When used thoughtfully, these substitutions can replace both the moisture and the flavor of fat.

To find out what works best for you, try some experimenting. Start by reducing the fat in a recipe by half and progressively reduce it further for as long as the taste remains intact. Also, try different substitutions until you find the one most satisfying to your taste.

In some cases, low-fat ingredients will bake more quickly so you may have to adjust baking times. Using a wooden toothpick, check the dessert ten minutes earlier than you normally would. If the toothpick comes out clean, you know the dessert is done.

The following table gives some easy substitutions to recondition those high-fat favorites into light, low-fat delights. Experiment with these until you find the best ingredient for your taste. In many instances, you may find that you prefer your new, low-fat creation.

Standard Ingredient	**Low-fat Substitute**
1 cup butter	1/2 cup fruit purée (applesauce, mashed banana, pitted prunes) & 2 tablespoons butter
1 cup oil	3/4 cup applesauce & 2 tablespoons oil or 1 cup molasses & 2 tablespoons oil (reduce sugar in recipe by 1 cup)
1 cup margarine	1/2 cup buttermilk or 1/2 cup nonfat yogurt
1 cup whole milk	1 cup nonfat milk or 1 cup buttermilk
1 whole egg	2 egg whites
2 eggs	2 egg whites plus 1 egg
1 cup sour cream	1 cup nonfat yogurt or nonfat sour cream
8 ounces cream cheese	8 ounces fat-free cream cheese or 1 cup strained yogurt
1/2 cup heavy cream	1/2 cup evaporated skim milk
1 ounce cooking chocolate	1 ounce unsweetened cocoa powder & 1 teaspoon water

Cakes & Cheesecakes

With these savvy recipes, you can enjoy the taste and texture of wonderfully delicious cakes without thinking twice. Low in fat and full of flavor, you *can* have your cake and eat it, too.

ALMOND SPONGE ROLL

A spiral of flavors and textures, this roll cake makes a wonderful presentation.

non-stick cooking spray
3 large eggs, separated, at room
   temperature
1 teaspoon vegetable oil
1 teaspoon vanilla extract
1/2 cup sugar, divided
1/3 cup cake flour, sifted
1/2 teaspoon cream of tartar

Filling
1/2 teaspoon almond extract
2 cups prepared low-fat vanilla pudding
1/4 cup nonfat chocolate syrup
confectioners sugar for garnish
mint leaves for garnish

Preheat oven to 425° F. Thoroughly spray an 11 x 17 x 1-inch jelly-roll pan with non-stick cooking spray. In a large bowl, blend egg yolks, oil, vanilla extract and 1/4 cup sugar. Beat until thick and creamy. Fold in flour.

In a very clean, medium-sized bowl, beat egg whites and cream of tartar. When soft peaks begin to form, sprinkle remaining sugar, 1 tablespoon at a time, into the egg whites. When egg whites are very stiff fold them into egg yolk mixture. Spread batter evenly in prepared pan and bake 6 to 10 minutes. The cake should be lightly browned and springy to the touch. With a knife, loosen the cake from edges of pan. Remove cake, inverting pan onto a towel.

While cake is still warm, mold it into a jelly-roll shape by rolling the cake and towel together from one narrow end to the other. The towel will give shape to the cake until the filling is added. Set aside.

Blend almond extract with vanilla pudding. Unroll the cake and remove the towel. Drizzle top of cake with chocolate syrup and then cover with pudding. Reroll and place on a platter. Sift confectioners sugar on top and garnish with mint leaves.

SERVES: 10	NUTRITIONAL INFORMATION PER SERVING				
Calories	112	Total Fat	2 g	Cholesterol	16 mg
Calories from Fat	16%	Saturated Fat	1 g	Sodium	48 mg

FRESH COCONUT CAKE

Despite its unhealthy reputation, fresh coconut contributes minimal fat and big tropical flavor to this recipe.

non-stick cooking spray
1/2 cup coconut milk
  (if you don't have 1/2 cup, make up
  the difference with water)
1/2 cup coconut meat, diced
1 cup 1% buttermilk
1 teaspoon baking soda

2 1/2 cups all-purpose flour
1 cup sugar
1/2 teaspoon baking powder
2 egg whites, whipped with a fork
1/3 cup corn syrup
1/4 cup vegetable oil
1 teaspoon coconut extract

Preheat oven to 350° F. Spray a 13 x 9 x 3-inch baking pan with non-stick cooking spray.

Hammer 2 or 3 holes into one side of coconut and drain milk into a cup, then smash coconut open to get to the meat. With a knife, cut coconut meat from shell. Dice coconut meat.

In a small bowl, blend buttermilk and baking soda and set aside. In a large bowl, combine flour, sugar and baking powder. Stir to blend.

In a medium-sized bowl, blend egg whites with corn syrup, vegetable oil and coconut extract. In a blender, process coconut milk with meat until very smooth. Fold all wet ingredients into dry ingredients. With an electric mixer, beat on low for 30 seconds, then beat on medium for 2 minutes. Pour into prepared baking pan. Bake 30 to 35 minutes or until a wooden toothpick inserted into the center of the cake comes out clean. Cool and cut into 16 servings.

SERVES: 16	NUTRITIONAL INFORMATION PER SERVING				
Calories	183	Total Fat	4 g	Cholesterol	< 1 mg
Calories from Fat	20%	Saturated Fat	1 g	Sodium	51 mg

WHITE CAKE

Makes a great base for fruit toppings, glossy frostings or both.

non-stick cooking spray
2 1/4 cups cake flour, sifted
2 teaspoons baking powder
3/4 teaspoon salt
1/2 cup light margarine
1 cup sugar
2 teaspoons vanilla extract
3 egg whites, at room temperature
1 cup 1% buttermilk

Frosting
1 1/4 cups sugar
1/3 cup water
2 egg whites, at room temperature
1/4 teaspoon cream of tartar
3 tablespoons confectioners
  sugar, sifted
1 teaspoon vanilla extract
1 cup sliced strawberries (optional)

Preheat oven to 375° F. Spray two 8-inch cake pans with non-stick cooking spray. In a medium-sized bowl, blend flour with baking powder and salt. In a large bowl, cream margarine with sugar and vanilla extract. Blend in egg whites, 1 at a time, beating vigorously after adding each one. Creamed mixture should be light and fluffy. Fold in buttermilk alternately with flour mixture. Divide between pans and bake 20 to 25 minutes or until a wooden toothpick inserted into the center of each cake comes out clean. Cool and remove from pans.

To make frosting, blend sugar with water in a medium-sized saucepan and bring to a boil. In a large bowl, beat egg whites until frothy, blending in cream of tartar. Sift confectioners sugar into egg whites and beat until stiff. Gradually incorporate a stream of the boiling sugar mixture into egg white mixture. Do this very slowly so that the hot mixture can be well-blended into the stiffly beaten egg whites. Continue beating for 8 minutes, until mixture becomes cool. Add the vanilla extract.

Place one of the cake layers top down on a cake plate and frost. Cover with remaining cake and frost top and sides. Garnish with strawberries.

SERVES: 12	NUTRITIONAL INFORMATION PER SERVING				
Calories	217	Total Fat	4 g	Cholesterol	< 1 mg
Calories from Fat	17%	Saturated Fat	< 1 g	Sodium	233 mg

BLACK FOREST CAKE

A beautiful and delicious dessert. Though it tastes great, the frozen whipped topping doesn't hold its peaks long so make it just before serving.

non-stick cooking spray
1 1/2 cups cake flour, sifted
3/4 cup sugar
1/4 cup cocoa powder
1 teaspoon baking soda
1 teaspoon vanilla extract
1/4 cup nonfat chocolate syrup
1 1/2 teaspoons white vinegar
3 egg whites, whipped with a fork

2 tablespoons vegetable oil
2/3 cup water
1 20-ounce can cherry pie filling

Frozen Whipped Topping
1 teaspoon vanilla extract
1 6-ounce can evaporated skim milk
2 tablespoons sugar

Preheat oven to 325°F. Spray a 9-inch round baking pan with non-stick cooking spray.

Pour evaporated milk into a metal bowl and chill in freezer along with hand or electric beaters. In a large bowl, blend flour, sugar, cocoa and baking soda. In a smaller bowl, combine vanilla extract, chocolate syrup, vinegar, egg whites, oil and water. Stir the wet ingredients into the dry ones, blending well. Pour into prepared pan and bake 15 to 20 minutes or until a wooden toothpick inserted into the center of the cake comes out clean. Once the cake has cooled, top it with cherry pie filling.

To make the frozen whipped topping, remove partially frozen evaporated milk and beaters from freezer. Add the sugar and vanilla extract and beat on high for about five minutes or until mixture is creamy and stiff. Just before serving, top cake with a dollop of the frozen topping. Additional frozen topping can be served on the side.

SERVES: 10	NUTRITIONAL INFORMATION PER SERVING		
Calories	193	Total Fat	3 g	Cholesterol	1 mg
Calories from Fat	11%	Saturated Fat	< 1 g	Sodium	108 mg

BLUEBERRY UPSIDE DOWN CAKE

People traditionally use pineapple in upside down cakes but blueberries are a wonderful variation. As the berries pop during baking, their juice is absorbed into the cake.

non-stick cooking spray
12 ounces frozen or fresh blueberries
2 tablespoons frozen juice concentrate (orange, apple, or pineapple), thawed
1 cup sugar, divided
1 3/4 cups all-purpose flour
1 1/2 teaspoons baking powder

2/3 cup nonfat milk
2 egg whites, whipped with a fork
1/3 cup vegetable oil
1 teaspoon vanilla extract
mint leaves (optional)
extra berries (optional)

Preheat oven to 350° F. Spray a 9-inch round baking pan with non-stick cooking spray.

In a medium-sized bowl, blend blueberries, juice concentrate and 2 tablespoons of the sugar. Set aside. In a large bowl, combine flour, baking powder and remaining sugar. In a small bowl, blend milk, egg whites, oil and vanilla extract . Mix into dry ingredients. Pour blueberry mixture into prepared pan, and top with batter. Bake 35 to 40 minutes or until a wooden toothpick inserted into the center of the cake comes out clean. Allow to cool.

With a knife, loosen the cake from the sides of the pan and invert onto a round serving platter. Garnish sides of platter with mint leaves and extra berries if desired.

SERVES: 8 ━━━━━━ **NUTRITIONAL INFORMATION PER SERVING** ━━━━━

Calories	183	Total Fat	4 g	Cholesterol	< 1 mg
Calories from Fat	19%	Saturated Fat	< 1 g	Sodium	58 mg

CHERRY STREUSEL CAKE

Cherry Streusel Cake could easily double as a coffeecake—not too sweet and with a light crumb.

non-stick cooking spray
3 tablespoons light margarine
1/3 cup corn syrup
1 cup sugar
1 cup nonfat milk
4 egg whites, whipped with a fork
2 teaspoons vanilla extract

2 1/4 cups all-purpose flour, divided
2 teaspoons baking powder
1 teaspoon baking soda
1 20-ounce can cherry pie filling
1/4 cup brown sugar
1 teaspoon cinnamon

Preheat oven to 325° F. Spray a 9-inch square pan with non-stick cooking spray.

In a large bowl, cream margarine with corn syrup and sugar. Add milk, egg whites and vanilla extract, blending thoroughly. In a medium-sized bowl, mix 2 cups of the flour with baking powder and baking soda. Blend wet ingredients into dry ingredients. Spread batter evenly into the prepared pan. Top with cherry pie filling.

In a small bowl, blend remaining flour (1/4 cup) with brown sugar and cinnamon. Sprinkle over the top of cake. Bake 55 to 60 minutes or until a wooden toothpick inserted into the center of the cake comes out clean. Cool. Cut into 12 squares and serve.

SERVES: 12 ═══════════ **NUTRITIONAL INFORMATION PER SERVING** ═══════════

Calories	202	Total Fat	1 g	Cholesterol	< 1 mg
Calories from Fat	6%	Saturated Fat	< 1 g	Sodium	148 mg

POPPY CUPS

The perfect accompaniment to a steaming mug of coffee.

30 baking cups (60 for mini-cupcakes)
1/3 cup poppy seeds
2 3/4 cups all-purpose flour
2 teaspoons baking powder
1 teaspoon baking soda
1 teaspoon salt

1/4 cup light margarine
1/4 cup corn syrup
1 1/2 cups sugar
1 1/2 teaspoons vanilla extract
4 egg whites, whipped with a fork
1 1/4 cups 1% buttermilk

Preheat oven to 375° F. Line 30 muffin tins or 60 mini-muffin tins with baking cups.

Bring one cup of water to a boil and add poppy seeds. Remove from heat and soak poppy seeds for one hour. Line a tea strainer with a paper towel and drain the poppy seeds.

In a medium-sized bowl, combine flour, baking powder, baking soda and salt.

In a large bowl, cream margarine with corn syrup, sugar and vanilla extract. Add eggs, creaming to a smooth mixture. Alternately add buttermilk and dry ingredients to creamed mixture. Fold in poppy seeds. Fill baking cups 2/3 full. Bake regular-sized cupcakes 15 to 18 minutes (8- 10 minutes for mini-cupcakes).

Makes 30 regular or 60 mini cupcakes

1 PER SERVING ══════ **NUTRITIONAL INFORMATION PER SERVING*** ══════

Calories	91	Total Fat	2 g	Cholesterol	< 1 mg
Calories from Fat	16%	Saturated Fat	< 1 g	Sodium	154 mg

* Nutritional information is based on regular-sized cupcakes

LEMON CREAM CAKE

🕐 *A light and satisfying bundt cake.*

non-stick cooking spray
2 cups all-purpose flour
1 teaspoon baking powder
4 ounces fat-free cream cheese
1/2 cup sugar
1/4 cup corn syrup
4 egg whites, whipped with a fork
1/4 cup vegetable oil

2 tablespoons freshly squeezed
  lemon juice
1/2 teaspoon vanilla extract
1 cup nonfat yogurt

Icing
1 cup confectioners sugar, sifted
7 teaspoons nonfat milk
lemon zest for garnish

Preheat oven to 350° F. Spray a 10-inch bundt pan with non-stick cooking spray.

In a large bowl, mix flour and baking powder. Set aside.

In a medium-sized bowl, cream the fat-free cream cheese, sugar, corn syrup, egg whites, vegetable oil, lemon juice and vanilla extract. Stir in yogurt. Fold creamed mixture into dry mixture and pour into prepared pan. Bake 35 to 40 minutes or until a wooden toothpick inserted into the center of the cake comes out clean. Cool.

To make icing, blend confectioners sugar with milk. After cake has cooled, drizzle top with icing and garnish with lemon zest.

SERVES: 16	NUTRITIONAL INFORMATION PER SERVING		
Calories	166	Total Fat	4 g	Cholesterol	1 mg
Calories from Fat	20%	Saturated Fat	< 1 g	Sodium	56 mg

APPLE CAKE

🕐 *Here's a cake you'll want to make just to smell it baking.*

non-stick cooking spray
5 medium apples, peeled and chopped
2 teaspoons cinnamon
2 1/2 cups flour
1/2 cup sugar
2 teaspoons baking soda

3/4 cup corn syrup
6 egg whites, whipped lightly
   with a fork
1/2 teaspoon vanilla extract
1/2 cup raisins, plumped by steaming
   over boiling water for 5 minutes

Preheat oven to 350° F. Spray a 13 x 9 x 3-inch baking pan with non-stick cooking spray.

In a medium-sized bowl, combine apples with cinnamon. Set aside. In a large bowl, blend flour, sugar and baking soda. Add corn syrup, egg whites and vanilla extract. Fold in raisins and cinnamon-apple mixture. Pour into prepared pan and bake 40 to 45 minutes or until a wooden toothpick inserted into the center of the cake comes out clean.

Cool and cut into 16 pieces.

SERVES: 16 ═══════ **NUTRITIONAL INFORMATION PER SERVING** ═══════

Calories	182	Total Fat	< 1 g	Cholesterol	0 mg
Calories from Fat	2%	Saturated Fat	< 1 g	Sodium	136 mg

CHOCOLATE DEVIL'S FOOD CAKE

This recipe originated in the Pennsylvania Dutch area. With just three grams of fat, it's a delicious calorie bargain.

non-stick cooking spray
6 tablespoons light margarine
1 cup sugar
1/4 cup corn syrup
4 egg whites, whipped with a fork
1 teaspoon vanilla extract
1/4 cup cocoa powder
3 tablespoons hot coffee
2 cups cake flour, sifted
1 teaspoon salt

1 teaspoon baking soda
1 cup 1% buttermilk

Frosting
2 tablespoons light margarine
3/4 cup brown sugar, packed
1/4 cup evaporated skim milk
1 1/2 cups confectioners sugar
1 teaspoon vanilla extract

Preheat oven to 350° F. Spray a 13 x 9 x 3-inch baking pan with non-stick cooking spray.

Cream margarine with sugar, corn syrup, egg whites and vanilla extract. In a separate bowl, mix cocoa and hot coffee to make a smooth paste, then add to the creamed mixture.

In a large bowl, combine flour, salt and baking soda. Alternately add buttermilk and creamed cocoa mixture, blending well. Pour into prepared pan. Bake 35 to 40 minutes or until a toothpick inserted in the middle of the cake comes out clean. Cool.

To make frosting, melt margarine with brown sugar and evaporated milk. Heat and stir until sugar dissolves. Cool slightly then add confectioners sugar and vanilla extract.

Frost cake after it has cooled.

SERVES: 16 ═══════ **NUTRITIONAL INFORMATION PER SERVING** ═══════

Calories	232	Total Fat	3 g	Cholesterol	< 1 mg
Calories from Fat	12%	Saturated Fat	< 1 g	Sodium	284 mg

CHOCOLATE ANGEL CAKE WITH RASPBERRY FILLING

Two different raspberry flavors add zest to this delicious angel cake. Though the preparation is time-consuming, the results are exquisite.

1 cup cake flour, sifted
1 cup confectioners sugar, sifted
1/4 cup cocoa powder
12 large egg whites,
   at room temperature
1/2 teaspoon cream of tartar
1/4 teaspoon salt

1 cup sugar
1/2 teaspoon almond extract
1 3-ounce package raspberry
   gelatin dessert
2 cups water
1 12-ounce package frozen
   raspberries, thawed

Preheat oven to 375 ° F. You will need a 10-inch tube pan. Do not use non-stick spray so that the cake will be able to rise easily up the sides of the pan.

In a medium-sized bowl, sift cake flour with confectioners sugar and cocoa powder. Set aside.

In a large mixing bowl, use electric mixer to whip egg whites with cream of tartar and salt until the mixture is foamy. Sift sugar, 2 tablespoons at a time, into egg whites, continuing to whip on high speed until stiff peaks form. Make sure all sugar has been incorporated into the egg whites. (You can tell this by pinching a bit of the whipped egg white between your fingers. If sugar has been incorporated, you will feel no grains.)

Fold in the almond extract. Add flour mixture, about 1/4 cup at a time, to whipped egg whites. Fold in gently until just blended.

Place batter into the tube pan. Cut gently through the batter with a knife to remove any large bubbles. Bake 45 minutes or until crust is golden brown and cracks are very dry. Remove cake from the oven and invert it to cool for 1 hour.

With a knife, loosen sides and bottom of cake from pan. Remove it carefully.

Evenly cut off top 1 inch of cake and put it gently to the side. Carefully hollow out the base of the cake.

Blend gelatin dessert with 1 cup boiling water to dissolve. When dissolved, add 1 cup cold water containing two ice cubes in it. When gelatin begins to stiffen, spoon into hollowed cake. Replace top of cake and refrigerate 1 hour.

Before serving, blend frozen raspberries into a purée and pour onto serving plates. Place each slice of cake in the middle of the purée.

SERVES: 12 ======= **NUTRITIONAL INFORMATION PER SERVING** =======

Calories	193	Total Fat	1 g	Cholesterol	0 mg
Calories from Fat	4%	Saturated Fat	< 1 g	Sodium	113 mg

DAFFODIL CAKE

This cake is high, tender and moist like angel food. With alternating patches of yellow and white batter, it has a flower-like appearance.

White Cake Batter
1/4 cup plus 1 tablespoon cake
  flour, sifted
1/4 cup confectioners sugar, sifted
6 large egg whites, at room temperature
1/2 teaspoon cream of tartar
1/8 teaspoon salt
1/2 cup sugar

Yellow Cake Batter
1/4 cup plus 1 tablespoon cake
  flour, sifted
1/4 cup confectioners sugar, sifted
1 teaspoon lemon extract
2 egg yolks
6 large egg whites, at room temperature
1/2 teaspoon cream of tartar
1/8 teaspoon salt
1 cup sugar

Preheat oven to 325 ° F. Prepare a 10-inch tube pan by cleaning it well. Do not use non-stick cooking spray so that the cake will be able to rise easily up the sides of the pan.

To make white cake batter, in a medium-sized bowl, sift cake flour with confectioners sugar. Set aside. In a large mixing bowl, whip egg whites with cream of tartar and salt until the mixture is foamy. Sift sugar, 2 tablespoons at a time, into egg whites, continuing to whip on high speed until stiff peaks form. Make sure sugar has been incorporated into the egg whites. (You can tell this by pinching a bit of the whipped egg white between your fingers. If sugar has been incorporated, you will feel no grains.) Add flour mixture, about 1/4 cup at a time, to whipped egg whites. Fold in gently until just blended.

To make yellow cake batter, in a medium-sized bowl, sift cake flour with confectioners sugar. Set aside. In a small bowl, beat lemon extract and egg yolks until thick and lemon colored. In a large bowl combine egg whites, cream of tartar and salt. Whip until foamy. Sift sugar, 2 tablespoons at a time, into egg whites, continuing to whip on high speed until stiff peaks form. Make sure sugar has been incorporated into the egg whites. Add yolk mixture, folding in for 35 or 40 strokes. Carefully fold in flour mixture.

Drop alternating spoonfuls of batter into pan, creating a chain of yellow and white pockets of cake. Bake for 1 hour or until cake springs back when pressed in the middle. Invert the pan until cool. Loosen sides and bottom of cake and carefully remove from pan.

SERVES: 12 ═══════════ **NUTRITIONAL INFORMATION PER SERVING** ═══════════

| Calories | 180 | Total Fat | 1 g | Cholesterol | 35 mg |
| Calories from Fat | 5% | Saturated Fat | < 1 g | Sodium | 101 mg |

POUND CAKE

🕐 *Sliced pound cake makes a great base for sauces, fresh fruit and nonfat frozen yogurts.*

non-stick cooking spray
2 1/2 cups flour
1 teaspoon baking powder
1/2 cup light margarine
1/4 cup corn syrup

1 cup sugar
4 egg whites
1 cup nonfat vanilla yogurt
2 teaspoons vanilla extract

Preheat oven to 350° F. Spray a 9 x 5 x 3-inch loaf pan with non-stick cooking spray.

In a large bowl, sift flour with baking powder. In a medium-sized bowl, cream margarine with corn syrup, sugar, egg whites, yogurt and vanilla extract. Fold the creamed mixture into the dry mixture until very smooth. Pour into prepared pan. Bake 50 to 55 minutes or until a wooden toothpick inserted into the center of the cake comes out clean. Cool.

Run a knife around the sides before removing cake from pan. Cut into 16 slices.

SERVES: 16 ══ **NUTRITIONAL INFORMATION PER SERVING** ══

Calories	166	Total Fat	3 g	Cholesterol	< 1 mg
Calories from Fat	16%	Saturated Fat	< 1 g	Sodium	111 mg

MOCHA "SOUR CREAM" CAKE

A yogurt based topping complements this rich coffee and chocolate-flavored cake.

non-stick cooking spray
1 cup nonfat sour cream
1 tablespoon very strong, cold coffee
2 tablespoons vegetable oil
1/2 cup cocoa powder
1 cup all-purpose flour
1 teaspoon baking powder
1 teaspoon baking soda
1 cup sugar, divided

6 egg whites, at room temperature
1/2 teaspoon cream of tartar

Topping
1 cup nonfat yogurt, coffee flavor
1/4 cup cocoa powder
1 cup low-fat frozen whipped
  topping, thawed

Preheat oven to 350° F. Spray an 8-inch springform pan with non-stick cooking spray.

In a small bowl, blend sour cream, coffee and oil. In medium-sized bowl, blend cocoa, flour, baking powder, baking soda and 2/3 cup sugar. Add sour cream mixture to flour mixture and blend well.

In a large, very clean bowl, beat egg whites and cream of tartar until frothy. When soft peaks begin to form, sprinkle remaining sugar, 1 tablespoon at a time, into the egg whites. Add the flour mixture, a little at a time, until well-blended. Bake in prepared pan for 50 to 55 minutes. Cake should be evenly browned and spring back when touched lightly in the center. When cool, remove from pan. Place on a serving platter.

To make topping, blend yogurt with whipped topping and cocoa powder. Spread over cake and refrigerate for 2 hours.

SERVES: 8 ══════ **NUTRITIONAL INFORMATION PER SERVING** ══════

Calories	183	Total Fat	3 g	Cholesterol	1 mg
Calories from Fat	16%	Saturated Fat	< 1 g	Sodium	178 mg

SPICED CARROT CAKE

While lowering the fat content of traditional carrot cake, this recipe still produces a moist cake with great flavor.

non-stick cooking spray
2 1/2 cups all-purpose flour
1 teaspoon baking powder
1 teaspoon baking soda
1 teaspoon cinnamon
1 teaspoon allspice
1 cup sugar
1/2 cup light margarine
1/3 cup corn syrup
1/3 cup apple juice
1 teaspoon vanilla extract

3 egg whites, whipped with a fork
1 cup raisins, plumped by steaming
  over boiling water for 5 minutes
1 cup peeled, shredded carrots

Icing
1 1/2 cups fat-free cream cheese
1 teaspoon vanilla extract
1 cup confectioners sugar
carrot shreds for garnish

Preheat oven to 325° F. Spray a 13 x 9 x 3-inch baking pan with non-stick cooking spray.

In a large mixing bowl, blend flour with baking powder, baking soda, cinnamon and allspice.

In a medium-sized bowl, cream margarine with sugar, corn syrup, apple juice, vanilla extract and egg whites. Mix into dry ingredients. Fold in raisins and carrots. Pour into prepared pan and bake 35 to 45 minutes. Cool.

To prepare icing, mix cream cheese with vanilla extract and confectioners sugar. Spread icing onto cooled cake and garnish with a few carrot shreds.

SERVES: 16 ══════════ NUTRITIONAL INFORMATION PER SERVING ═══════════

| Calories | 211 | Total Fat | 3 g | Cholesterol | < 1 mg |
| Calories from Fat | 13% | Saturated Fat | < 1 g | Sodium | 162 mg |

LEMON PINWHEELS

In this recipe, the double lemon flavor and the hint of chocolate produce a deliciously different dessert.

non-stick cooking spray
3 large eggs, separated,
   at room temperature
1 teaspoon vegetable oil
1/2 cup sugar, divided
1 tablespoon freshly squeezed
   lemon juice

1/3 cup cake flour, sifted
1/2 teaspoon cream of tartar
1/4 cup nonfat chocolate syrup
2 cups prepared fat-free lemon pudding
confectioners sugar for garnish
lemon zest for garnish

Preheat oven to 425° F. Thoroughly spray the bottom of an 11 x 17-inch jelly-roll pan with non-stick cooking spray. In a large bowl, blend egg yolks, oil, 1/4 cup sugar and lemon juice. Beat until thick and creamy. Fold in flour.

In a very clean, medium-sized bowl, beat egg whites and cream of tartar. When soft peaks begin to form, sprinkle remaining sugar, 1 tablespoon at a time, into the egg whites. When egg whites are very stiff fold them into egg yolk mixture. Spread batter evenly in prepared pan and bake 6 to 10 minutes. The cake should be lightly browned and springy to the touch. With a knife, loosen the cake from edges of pan. Remove cake, inverting pan onto a large towel. While cake is still warm, mold it into a jelly-roll shape by rolling the cake and towel together from one narrow end to the other. The towel will give shape to the cake until the filling is added. Set aside.

Prepare lemon pudding according to package directions.

Unroll the cake and remove the towel. Sprinkle the top of cake with chocolate syrup and then cover with lemon pudding. Reroll and place on a platter. Top with a little sifted confectioners sugar and lemon zest.

SERVES: 10 ═══════ **NUTRITIONAL INFORMATION PER SERVING** ═══════

Calories	122	Total Fat	2 g	Cholesterol	65 mg
Calories from Fat	15%	Saturated Fat	1 g	Sodium	49 mg

TRIPLE RIPPLE CAKE

Combines the flavors of chocolate and raspberry with a delicate icing.

non-stick cooking spray
1 1/4 cups 1% buttermilk
1 teaspoon baking soda
1/2 cup light margarine
1 1/4 cups sugar
4 egg whites
3 cups all-purpose flour
1 cup frozen raspberries, thawed

2 tablespoons cocoa powder
1-2 teaspoons warm water

Icing
1 cup confectioners sugar, sifted
4 teaspoons nonfat milk
1 teaspoon vanilla extract

Preheat oven to 350° F. Spray a 10-inch tube pan with non-stick cooking spray.

In a small bowl, mix buttermilk with baking soda and set aside.

In a large bowl, blend margarine, sugar and egg whites. Beat until light, frothy and well-blended. Gradually add buttermilk mixture and flour, beating until well-blended.

Remove two 3/4 cup portions of batter, placing them in separate bowls. In a blender, finely purée raspberries. Fold into one of the 3/4 cup portions of cake batter. Fold cocoa into the other portion of batter. If the cocoa batter is too stiff, add 1 or 2 teaspoons of warm water.

Place 1 cup plain batter into tube pan, keeping it contained in a "pocket" instead of spreading it into a layer. Next to this pocket of plain batter, place a one-cup scoop of the raspberry batter, then another cup of plain batter, followed by a one-cup scoop of the chocolate batter. Continue this alternating pattern until all batter is used up. Draw a knife through the batters to create a ripple effect.

Bake 30 to 35 minutes or until a wooden toothpick inserted into the center of the cake comes out clean. Cool.

To make icing, blend sifted confectioners sugar with nonfat milk and vanilla extract. Before serving, run a knife around the sides of pan, invert and gently tap to release cake. Drizzle icing on top of cake and down the sides.

SERVES: 16 ═══ **NUTRITIONAL INFORMATION PER SERVING** ═══

Calories	208	Total Fat	3 g	Cholesterol	< 1 mg
Calories from Fat	14%	Saturated Fat	< 1 g	Sodium	111 mg

STREUSEL CAKE

This is a wonderful cake to serve with coffee or tea.

non-stick cooking spray
3/4 cup 1% buttermilk
2 teaspoon baking soda
1 1/2 cups oatmeal
2 cups all-purpose flour, divided

1 1/4 cups sugar, divided
1/2 cup corn syrup, divided
1 1/2 cups applesauce
2 teaspoons vanilla extract
1/4 cup vegetable oil

Preheat oven to 325° F. Spray a 13 x 9 x 3-inch baking pan with non-stick cooking spray.

In a small bowl, blend buttermilk with baking soda and set aside. In a medium-sized bowl, blend oatmeal with 1/4 cup flour, 1/4 cup sugar and 1/4 cup corn syrup. Set aside.

In a large bowl, combine remaining flour with remaining sugar. Add applesauce, vanilla extract, remaining corn syrup, oil and buttermilk mixture. Blend well. Pour into prepared pan. Top with oatmeal mixture.

Bake 45 to 50 minutes or until a wooden toothpick inserted into the center of the cake comes out clean. Cool. Cut into 20 squares and serve.

SERVES: 20 ═══ **NUTRITIONAL INFORMATION PER SERVING** ═══

Calories	175	Total Fat	3 g	Cholesterol	< 1 mg
Calories from Fat	16%	Saturated Fat	< 1 g	Sodium	93 mg

STARS AND STRIPES SHORTCAKE

Using fresh raspberries, strawberries and blueberries, Stars and Stripes Shortcake makes for a delicious salute to the red, white and blue on patriotic holidays.

non-stick cooking spray
6 cups assorted fresh berries
   (raspberries, strawberries,
   blueberries), washed
1/4 cup plus 3 tablespoons granulated
   sugar, divided

3 cups all-purpose flour
1 tablespoon baking powder
1/2 teaspoon salt
1/2 cup light margarine
2 large egg whites
2/3 cup nonfat milk

Preheat oven to 450 ° F. Spray a cookie sheet with non-stick cooking spray. Combine berries with 1/4 cup sugar and set aside for 30 minutes at room temperature.

Meanwhile, combine flour, 2 tablespoons sugar, baking powder and salt. Cut the margarine into the flour mixture with a pastry blender or a fork until the mixture takes on a coarse, crumb texture. In a separate bowl, combine egg whites and milk. Add to flour mixture, stirring until flour is just moistened.

Powder a cutting board with a little flour. Using a rolling pin, roll the shortcake dough to 1/2 inch thickness. With a medium-sized, star-shaped cookie cutter, cut 24 stars (or whatever shapes you desire). Try to keep dough scraps to a minimum, and reroll dough only once so that it does not toughen. Place stars on cookie sheet. Sprinkle with 1 tablespoon sugar.

Bake the stars for 10 minutes or until lightly browned and firm to the touch. Remove stars from cookie sheet and cool for 10 minutes on a wire rack. Place two stars in each serving bowl and cover with fruit.

SERVES: 12 ═══════ **NUTRITIONAL INFORMATION PER SERVING** ═══════

Calories	193	Total Fat	4 g	Cholesterol	< 1 mg
Calories from Fat	19%	Saturated Fat	< 1 g	Sodium	275 mg

SUNSHINE CAKE

A delicate and luscious sponge cake bursting with orange flavor.

1 1/2 cups cake flour, sifted
1/4 teaspoon salt
1 1/4 cups sugar, divided
3 eggs, separated
1/2 teaspoon lemon extract
1/2 teaspoon orange extract
1/4 cup corn syrup

6 egg whites, at room temperature
1 teaspoon cream of tartar

Icing
1 cup confectioners sugar
7 teaspoons orange juice

Preheat oven to 325° F. Prepare a 10-inch tube pan by cleaning thoroughly. Do not use non-stick cooking spray so that the cake will be able to rise easily up the sides of the pan.

In a medium-sized bowl, blend flour with salt and 1 cup sugar. Set aside.

In a separate bowl, use a hand beater or an electric mixer to beat egg yolks until thick and lemon colored. Beat in lemon extract, orange extract and corn syrup. Clean beaters. In a large, clean, warm bowl, beat egg whites and cream of tartar until just frothy. Sift remaining sugar into the egg whites, 1 tablespoon at a time, until it is all incorporated. (You can tell this by pinching a bit of the whipped egg white between your fingers. If sugar has been incorporated, you will feel no grains.) Continue beating egg whites until soft peaks form. Fold in egg yolk mixture first and then add flour mixture.

Pour into prepared pan. Bake for 1 hour or until the mixture springs back when touched. Invert pan until cool. When cool, run a knife around the edges of pan and gently remove cake onto a serving platter. To make icing, blend confectioners sugar with orange juice. Drizzle over cake.

SERVES: 15 ══════ **NUTRITIONAL INFORMATION PER SERVING** ══════

Calories	170	Total Fat	1 g	Cholesterol	43 mg
Calories from Fat	6%	Saturated Fat	< 1 g	Sodium	74 mg

TRIFLE

To save time, purchase an angel food cake and eliminate the first 7 ingredients!

1 cup cake flour, sifted
1 cup confectioners sugar, sifted
12 large egg whites,
  at room temperature
1/2 teaspoon cream of tartar
1/4 teaspoon salt
1 cup sugar
1/2 teaspoon almond extract
10 ounces fruit spread or preserves
2 16-ounce cans of fruit of your choice
  (peaches, apricots, cherries)
fresh fruit and mint for garnish

Pudding
1/4 cup all-purpose flour
2 tablespoons arrowroot
2 12-ounce cans evaporated skim milk
1/2 cup dry sherry (optional)
1/3 cup honey
2 teaspoons vanilla extract

Preheat oven to 375 ° F. Clean a 10-inch tube pan well. Do not use non-stick cooking spray so that the cake will be able to rise easily up the sides of the pan.

Sift cake flour with confectioners sugar. Set aside. Using an electric mixer and a large mixing bowl, whip egg whites with cream of tartar and salt until the mixture is foamy. Sift sugar, 2 tablespoons at a time, into egg whites, continuing to whip on high speed until stiff peaks form. Make sure all sugar has been incorporated into the egg whites. (You can tell this by pinching a bit of the whipped egg white between your fingers. If sugar has been incorporated, you will feel no grains.) Fold in the almond extract. Spoon cake flour mixture, 1/4 cup at a time, into whipped egg whites. Fold in gently until just blended.

Pour batter into tube pan. Cut gently through the batter with a knife to remove any large bubbles. Bake 45 minutes or until crust is golden brown and cracks are very dry. Remove cake from the oven and invert to cool for 1 hour. Loosen sides and bottom and remove from pan. Cut into 2 inch squares.

To make pudding, whisk flour, arrowroot, milk, sherry and honey in a medium saucepan. Bring mixture to a boil, reduce heat to low. Cook, stirring constantly, until mixture thickens and becomes creamy. This should take 8 to 10 minutes. Stir in vanilla extract, and allow to cool.

In a large glass bowl, make a layer of cake squares and cover with a third of the pudding, preserves and fruit. Arrange another layer of cake squares and cover with another third of pudding, preserves and fruit. Repeat these steps a third time to use all remaining ingredients.

Cover and refrigerate. Before serving, garnish with fresh fruit pieces and mint leaves.

SERVES: 12 ══════ **NUTRITIONAL INFORMATION PER SERVING** ══════

Calories	195	Total Fat	< 1 g	Cholesterol	1 mg
Calories from Fat	1%	Saturated Fat	< 1 g	Sodium	125 mg

FRIENDSHIP STARTER

Friendship Starter is the sourdough base for the Friendship Cake that follows.

1 package dry yeast, 1/4-ounce	2 cups all-purpose flour
2 cups very warm water, 115° F	cheese cloth

Combine yeast, water and flour in a large glass mixing bowl. Stir until the mixture is smooth. Cover the container with a cheese cloth and allow to stand at room temperature for at least 2 days. Stir several times a day.

The starter is ready to use when it is bubbly and has a slightly acidic odor. After removing the amount of starter needed for a particular sourdough recipe, you can replenish the batch by adding 1 cup flour and 1 cup warm water.

The starter may be refrigerated after it becomes bubbly. Simply cover and refrigerate. If you don't use the starter for 10 days, stir in 1/2 teaspoon of sugar.

If you store the starter at room temperature, cover it with a light cloth. Never store in a tightly-sealed container if the starter is at room temperature!

FRIENDSHIP CAKE

An irresistible and aromatic combination of sourdough cake and rich fall flavors.

non-stick cooking spray
1 1/2 cups Friendship Starter
  (see previous recipe)
3 tablespoons vegetable oil
1/3 cup applesauce
1/3 cup corn syrup
6 egg whites
2 teaspoons vanilla extract
2 cups all-purpose flour

1 cup sugar
2 teaspoons baking powder
1/2 teaspoon salt
1 1/2 teaspoons cinnamon
1 1/2 teaspoons baking soda
2 apples, cored, peeled and chopped
1/4 cup chocolate morsels
1/4 cup chopped walnuts, toasted

Preheat oven to 350° F. Spray a large bundt pan with non-stick cooking spray.

In a medium-sized bowl, gently combine Friendship Starter with oil, applesauce, corn syrup, egg whites and vanilla extract. In a large bowl, blend flour, sugar, baking powder, salt, cinnamon and baking soda. Fold wet ingredients into dry ingredients. Fold in apples, chocolate morsels and walnuts.

Pour into prepared pan. Bake 40 to 50 minutes. Cake is done baking when it pulls away from the sides of the pan. Allow cake to cool for 10 minutes before removing from pan.

SERVES: 18 ═══════ NUTRITIONAL INFORMATION PER SERVING ═══════

| Calories | 188 | Total Fat | 4 g | Cholesterol | 0 mg |
| Calories from Fat | 20% | Saturated Fat | 1 g | Sodium | 191 mg |

Cheesecakes

Scrumptious and satisfying, cheesecake is often the choice cake on the menu. Use the basic cheesecake as a starting place and experiment with different toppings and fillings, fruits and sauces. Try the following recipes which are low in fat yet high in flavor.

Cheesecake Crusts

CHEESECAKE CRUSTS: Each of the following cheesecake crusts fits a 9-inch springform pan that serves eight. Make your own variations by using your favorite low-fat cookies. Crusts and fillings are analyzed for nutritional content separately.

GRAHAM CRACKER CRUST

non-stick cooking spray
3 ounces graham crackers, crushed
2 tablespoons sugar
2 tablespoons corn syrup

1/2 teaspoon cinnamon
1 egg white
1 tablespoon light margarine

Preheat oven to 350° F. Prepare a 9-inch springform pan by spraying well with non-stick cooking spray. In a medium-sized bowl, combine all ingredients. Press into pan. Bake 10 minutes. Cool.

SINGLE CRUST		NUTRITIONAL INFORMATION PER SERVING			
Calories	71	Total Fat	1 g	Cholesterol	0 mg
Calories from Fat	13%	Saturated Fat	< 1 g	Sodium	87 mg

GRANOLA CRUST

non-stick cooking spray
1 1/2 cups nonfat plain
  granola, crushed
1/4 cup apple juice

1 tablespoon honey
1 tablespoon light margarine
1 egg white

Preheat oven to 325° F. Prepare a 9-inch springform pan by spraying well with non-stick cooking spray. In a medium-sized bowl, combine all ingredients. Press into pan. Bake 12 to 15 minutes.

SINGLE CRUST		NUTRITIONAL INFORMATION PER SERVING			
Calories	43	Total Fat	1 g	Cholesterol	0 mg
Calories from Fat	19%	Saturated Fat	< 1 g	Sodium	62 mg

CHOCOLATE COOKIE CRUST

non-stick cooking spray
2 cups nonfat chocolate cookies
  (30 small), crushed

2 tablespoons nonfat chocolate syrup
1 tablespoon fruit preserves
1 tablespoon light margarine

Prepare a 9-inch springform pan by spraying well with non-stick cooking spray. In a medium-sized bowl, combine all ingredients. Press into pan. Refrigerate until ready to use.

SINGLE CRUST ══════ **NUTRITIONAL INFORMATION PER SERVING** ══════

Calories	48	Total Fat	1 g	Cholesterol	0 mg
Calories from Fat	19%	Saturated Fat	< 1 g	Sodium	48 mg

GINGERSNAP CRUST

non-stick cooking spray
1 1/2 cups nonfat gingersnap cookies,
  broken into pieces (about 4 ounces)

1/2 cup ground dates or figs
  (grind in food processor)
1 tablespoon corn syrup
2 tablespoons light margarine

Process gingersnaps and dates with a steel blade in the food processor. Prepare a 9-inch springform pan by spraying well with non-stick cooking spray. In a medium-sized bowl, combine all ingredients. Press into pan. Refrigerate until ready to use.

SINGLE CRUST ══════ **NUTRITIONAL INFORMATION PER SERVING** ══════

Calories	45	Total Fat	1 g	Cholesterol	0 mg
Calories from Fat	18%	Saturated Fat	< 1 g	Sodium	58 mg

BASIC CHEESECAKE

Try experimenting with a basic, creamy cheesecake. Top with fruit, pie filling or add different flavorings of your choice.

1 15-ounce container nonfat
  ricotta cheese
1 8-ounce package fat-free cream cheese
2 egg whites, whipped with a fork
2 eggs

3/4 cup sugar
1/3 cup all-purpose flour
2 teaspoons vanilla extract
1 prepared cheesecake crust of your
  choice (see pages 39 & 40)

Preheat oven to 350° F. In a medium-sized mixing bowl, blend ricotta cheese with cream cheese, egg whites, eggs, sugar, flour and 2 teaspoons vanilla extract. Mix and blend until very smooth. Pour into prepared crust.

Bake 50 to 55 minutes or until center of the cake is just firm. Remove from the oven and cool for 5 minutes. Chill thoroughly in the refrigerator before serving.

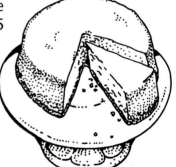

SERVES: 8 ===== **NUTRITIONAL INFORMATION PER SERVING*** =====

Calories	175	Total Fat	2 g	Cholesterol	55 mg
Calories from Fat	10%	Saturated Fat	1 g	Sodium	92 mg

* *Nutritional information is based on recipe made without crust.*

BLUEBERRY-FILLED CHEESECAKE

Blueberries are baked between two layers of scrumptious cheesecake batter.

1 15-ounce container nonfat
  ricotta cheese
1 8-ounce package fat-free cream cheese
2 egg whites, whipped with a fork
2 eggs
3/4 cup sugar, divided
1/3 cup all-purpose flour
1 teaspoon orange extract

1 prepared cheesecake crust
  of your choice (see pages 39 & 40)
2 cups fresh or frozen
  blueberries, drained
1/4 cup blueberry preserves
1/4 cup orange preserves
mint leaves and fresh blueberries
  for garnish

Preheat oven to 325° F. In a medium-sized mixing bowl, blend ricotta cheese, cream cheese, egg whites, eggs, 1/2 cup sugar, flour and orange extract. Blend until very smooth. Pour half the batter into prepared crust.

Mix blueberries with preserves and remaining sugar. Drop by spoonfuls over batter, reserving 1 large spoonful as garnish. Top with remaining half of cheesecake batter. Bake 60 to 70 minutes until the middle is just firm. Remove cake from oven.

When cool, remove from pan. Top with reserved blueberry mixture, a few mint leaves and blueberries.

SERVES: 8 ═══════ **NUTRITIONAL INFORMATION PER SERVING*** ═══════

Calories	171	Total Fat	2 g	Cholesterol	55 mg
Calories from Fat	10%	Saturated Fat	< 1 g	Sodium	111 mg

* Nutritional information is based on recipe made without crust

AMARETTO ESPRESSO CHEESECAKE

An elegant combination of nut and coffee flavors.

1/2 cup evaporated skim milk
1 16-ounce container nonfat
  ricotta cheese
2 8-ounce packages fat-free cream
  cheese, at room temperature
2 cups 1% buttermilk
1 1/2 cups granulated sugar, divided
4 whole eggs, separated
2 tablespoons lemon zest

1 1/2 cups flour
2 tablespoons Amaretto
2 tablespoons strong, cold espresso
4 egg whites, at room temperature
1 prepared cheesecake crust of your
  choice (see pages 39 & 40)
9-inch doily
confectioners sugar for garnish

Preheat oven to 425° F. Put evaporated milk in a small bowl and place in the freezer until ice crystals form around the edges of the bowl. In a large bowl, blend ricotta cheese and cream cheese with buttermilk. Gradually, beat in 1 cup sugar and egg yolks. Beat until thick. Stir in lemon zest, flour, Amaretto, and espresso.

In a separate bowl, use very clean beaters to beat all of the egg whites until foamy. Add remaining sugar, 1 tablespoon at a time, and continue to beat until the egg whites hold peaks. Beat the partially frozen evaporated milk until thick. Fold into egg whites, then fold this mixture into the cheese and buttermilk batter.

Pour into prepared crust. Smooth top. Bake 10 minutes. Lower oven temperature to 350° F and bake 60 minutes longer. Turn off heat in the oven and allow cake to cool with the oven door closed. When cool, cover and store in refrigerator. To serve, place doily over top of cooled cake. Sprinkle with confectioners sugar. Remove doily, and serve.

SERVES: 8 ═══════════ **NUTRITIONAL INFORMATION PER SERVING*** ═══════════

Calories	254	Total Fat	1 g	Cholesterol	43 mg
Calories from Fat	5%	Saturated Fat	< 1 g	Sodium	130 mg

* Nutritional information is based on recipe made without crust

LEMON CHEESECAKE

A tangy twist on a basic cheesecake turns it into a real refresher.

4 cups nonfat yogurt
1/3 cup all-purpose flour
3 tablespoons cornstarch
1 cup sugar
6 egg whites, whipped with a fork

1 teaspoon lemon extract
1 prepared cheesecake crust
  of your choice (see pages 39 & 40)
thin lemon slices for garnish

Preheat oven to 300° F. Drain yogurt in a strainer for a few minutes to remove most of the liquid. With an electric mixer, beat yogurt with flour, cornstarch and sugar. Beat until very smooth. Add egg whites, 2 at a time, and beat on high. Fold in lemon extract.

Pour into prepared crust. Bake 60 to 70 minutes or until the center of the cheesecake is just firm. Allow to cool.

Garnish with lemon slices. Store in the refrigerator until thoroughly chilled.

SERVES: 8	NUTRITIONAL INFORMATION PER SERVING*			
Calories	189	Total Fat	< 1 g	Cholesterol < 1 mg
Calories from Fat	2%	Saturated Fat	< 1 g	Sodium 121 mg

* Nutritional information is based on recipe made without crust

CHOCOLATE CHEESECAKE

A double dose of indulgence with just two grams of fat.

1/4 cup cocoa powder
3 8-ounce packages fat-free cream
   cheese, at room temperature
3/4 cup sugar
2 egg whites, whipped with a fork

1 egg
1 teaspoon vanilla extract
1 prepared cheesecake crust
   of your choice (see pages 39 & 40)

Preheat oven to 325° F.

In a medium-sized bowl, combine cocoa powder with cream cheese. Blend well. Add sugar, egg whites, egg and vanilla extract. Pour into prepared crust. Bake 40 to 50 minutes until the center of the cheesecake is just firm.

Cool thoroughly. Refrigerate until ready to serve.

SERVES: 8 ═══════ **NUTRITIONAL INFORMATION PER SERVING*** ═══════

Calories	124	Total Fat	2 g	Cholesterol	30 mg
Calories from Fat	15%	Saturated Fat	< 1 g	Sodium	92 mg

* Nutritional information is based on recipe made without crust

Pies & Tarts

With their short crusts and rich fillings, pies
have long been excluded from healthy diets.
The following recipes create new crusts and
reinvent traditional fillings, yielding savory pies
and tarts that fit into a healthy nutrition profile.

Pie Crusts

The crusts used for cheesecakes (see Cakes & Cheesecakes Chapter, pages 39-40) may also be used for the baked or unbaked pies in this chapter. The following are several more recipes for healthy pie crusts. Each single pie crust serves eight.

MERINGUE CRUST

A great pie shell for Fresh Strawberry Pie, Irish Coffee Pie, Chocolate Sundae Pie or Blueberry Cheesecake Pie.

non-stick cooking spray	1/2 cup sugar
2 egg whites, at room temperature	1/2 teaspoon salt
1/2 teaspoon cream of tartar	1/2 teaspoon vanilla extract

Preheat oven to 300° F. Spray a 9-inch pie plate with non-stick cooking spray.

In a medium-sized mixing bowl, use an electric beater to whip egg whites with cream of tartar and salt. When mixture is foamy, sift sugar, 1 tablespoon at a time, into egg whites, continuing to whip on high speed until stiff peaks form. Make sure all sugar has been incorporated into the egg whites. (You can tell this by pinching a bit of the whipped egg white between your fingers. If sugar has been incorporated, you will feel no grains.) Fold in the vanilla extract. Spread mixture onto the bottom and sides of prepared pan. To form a shell, build up the sides with a spoon.

Bake 50 minutes. Turn off oven and let the crust rest for 2 hours. Cool before filling.

SINGLE CRUST ═══════ **NUTRITIONAL INFORMATION PER SERVING** ═══════

Calories	47	Total Fat	0 g	Cholesterol	0 mg
Calories from Fat	0%	Saturated Fat	0 g	Sodium	147 mg

FILO DOUGH PIE CRUST

This recipe makes a delicious bottom crust. To add a top crust after you have made your pie, cover filling with two more sheets of filo, trim to fit pan and bake for time designated in pie recipe.

2 sheets frozen filo, defrosted and
  wrapped in damp dish towel

non-stick cooking spray

Preheat oven to 375° F. Remove a sheet of filo from damp towel. Fold in half and place across 9-inch pie plate. Spray a little non-stick cooking spray on filo. Repeat with second sheet of filo. Trim to fit. Prebake for 10 minutes or until shell is golden brown.

SINGLE CRUST		NUTRITIONAL INFORMATION PER SERVING			
Calories	17	Total Fat	< 1 g	Cholesterol	4 mg
Calories from Fat	1%	Saturated Fat	0 g	Sodium	< 1 mg

CRUNCHY CEREAL CRUST

This crust works for baked and chilled pies. It has a nice, crunchy texture.

non-stick cooking spray
5 cups whole-grain cereal flakes
2 tablespoons sugar

1 1/2 tablespoons butter
1 egg white, whipped with a fork

Preheat oven to 375° F. Spray a 9-inch pie plate with non-stick cooking spray.

Crush cereal in a food processor fitted with a steel knife or in a plastic bag with a rolling pin. Combine crushed cereal with sugar, butter and egg white. Blend well and press into pie plate with clean, wet fingers. Bake 10 minutes.

SINGLE CRUST		NUTRITIONAL INFORMATION PER SERVING			
Calories	20	Total Fat	< 1 g	Cholesterol	< 1 mg
Calories from Fat	< 1%	Saturated Fat	< 1 g	Sodium	27 mg

TRADITIONAL PIE CRUST

Not the fat-laden crust you've learned to avoid. Full of flavor, yet low in fat, this crust works well with many recipes.

non-stick cooking spray
1 1/2 to 2 cups all-purpose flour
1/3 cup sugar
1/2 teaspoon salt

2 tablespoons corn syrup
2 tablespoons vegetable oil
1 egg white, whipped with a fork
1/3 cup 1% buttermilk, very cold

Preheat oven to 400° F. Spray a 9-inch pie plate with non-stick cooking spray. Combine flour, sugar and salt in a medium-sized bowl making a well in the middle. In a separate bowl, blend corn syrup with vegetable oil and egg white. Pour into flour well and blend with a pastry blender or with two knives until mixture is crumbly. Pour half of the cold buttermilk over mixture and toss with a fork just until milk is absorbed. If the mixture seems too dry, add a little more buttermilk. Roll dough into a ball.

Put well-floured waxed paper on counter. Flatten ball on wax paper and flour the ball. Top with a second sheet of waxed paper. With a rolling pin, roll dough to approximate size of pie plate. Remove top piece of waxed paper and flip pastry onto pie plate. Fit pastry to pie plate and remove second piece of waxed paper. Flute edges of pastry. Bake 10 to 12 minutes or until well-browned.

SINGLE CRUST ══════ **NUTRITIONAL INFORMATION PER SERVING** ══════

Calories	152	Total Fat	3 g	Cholesterol	< 1 mg
Calories from Fat	20%	Saturated Fat	< 1 g	Sodium	27 mg

IRISH COFFEE PIE

Simple to make and a delectable treat. If you don't want to use spirits, replace with almond flavoring.

1 6-ounce can evaporated skim milk
1 tablespoon gelatin
1/3 cup water, cold
3/4 cup sugar, divided
1/8 teaspoon salt
3 teaspoons brewed coffee,
   very strong
1 egg

1/4 cup nonfat milk
2 tablespoons Irish Whiskey
   or Amaretto
1/4 cup slivered almonds, toasted
1 single crust pie shell, baked
   (Meringue Crust works well.
   See page 48.)

Place evaporated milk in a medium-sized bowl in the freezer along with beaters. Chill until ice crystals form around edges of bowl.

Soak gelatin in cold water until soft. Place in the top of a double boiler with very hot water in the bottom. Melt softened gelatin over the hot water. Remove from heat. Add 1/2 cup plus 2 tablespoons sugar, salt, coffee, egg, milk and Irish Whiskey. Mix well. Chill until mixture is syrupy.

Remove bowl of evaporated milk from freezer and whip milk with remaining sugar until mixture is thick and holds peaks. Add gelatin mixture while beating vigorously, as the cold mixture will cause the gelatin to harden. Fold in almonds reserving a few for garnish. Pour into pie shell, garnish with almonds and freeze for at least 2 hours.

SERVES: 8 ═══════ **NUTRITIONAL INFORMATION PER SERVING*** ═══════

Calories	131	Total Fat	2 g	Cholesterol	1 mg
Calories from Fat	7%	Saturated Fat	< 1 g	Sodium	81 mg

* Nutritional information is based on recipe made with Meringue Crust.

FRESH STRAWBERRY PIE

A beautiful dessert with only four ingredients. It can be made with any berry.

1 quart strawberries
3/4 cup sugar
1 envelope unflavored gelatin

1 single crust pie shell (Traditional
    Crust works well. See page 50.)

Wash and hull the strawberries. Remove 1 cup of the smallest berries for purée. Purée these berries in food processor or blender until smooth in consistency. In a sauce pan, bring strawberry purée and sugar to a boil. Boil 3 minutes, until all sugar is dissolved. Remove from heat.

Soften the gelatin in 1/4 cup water and then blend with hot strawberry purée. Beat with electric beater or with a whisk until the mixture is smooth and thick.

Place whole strawberries in the baked pie shell, turning down tops where caps were removed. Carefully, pour hot purée over strawberries, coating all fresh berries. Refrigerate 4 hours before serving.

SERVES: 8	NUTRITIONAL INFORMATION PER SERVING*				
Calories	177	Total Fat	4 g	Cholesterol	< 1 mg
Calories from Fat	20%	Saturated Fat	1 g	Sodium	17 mg

* Nutritional information is based on recipe made with Traditional Crust.

LEMON MERINGUE PIE

A Traditional Crust is a guarantee for a distinctive lemon meringue pie.

1 single crust pie shell, baked
   (Traditional Crust works well.
   See page 50.)
1 teaspoon lemon zest
1/3 cup freshly squeezed lemon juice
1/4 cup cornstarch
2 tablespoons all-purpose flour

1 2/3 cups sugar, divided
1/4 teaspoon salt
1 1/2 cups boiling water
3 eggs, separated
2 tablespoons butter
1/2 teaspoon cream of tartar

Preheat oven to 350° F. Sprinkle pie shell with lemon zest. In a medium saucepan, combine lemon juice with cornstarch, flour, 1 1/3 cups sugar and salt. Stir in boiling water. Cook over low heat, whisking constantly until thick and clear, about 3 minutes. Beat a little of the hot mixture into the egg yolks, then gently fold yolks into the hot mixture, stirring constantly. When mixture is thick and smooth, stir in the butter, allowing it to melt as you stir. Pour into the prepared pie shell.

Place egg whites and cream of tartar in a medium-sized, clean bowl and beat until frothy. Sift remaining sugar into the egg whites, 1 tablespoon at a time, until all sugar is incorporated. (You can tell this by pinching a bit of the whipped egg white between your fingers. If sugar has been incorporated, you will feel no grains.) Spread meringue lightly over the pie so that it touches all edges. Swirl to make peaks. Bake 12 to 15 minutes or until lightly browned. Cool at least 2 hours before cutting.

SERVES: 10 ══════ **NUTRITIONAL INFORMATION PER SERVING*** ══════

Calories	292	Total Fat	6 g	Cholesterol	70 mg
Calories from Fat	20%	Saturated Fat	2 g	Sodium	109 mg

* Nutritional information is based on recipe made with Traditional Crust.

POACHED PEARS WITH PRESERVES

Available almost every season, use fresh pears in this special dessert.

10 large, firm pears such as Anjou
1 teaspoon whole cloves
1 cup dry Marsala wine
1 stick cinnamon

1/2 cup brown sugar, packed
2 tablespoons cinnamon candies
1/2 cup raspberry preserves
mint sprigs for garnish

Peel pears leaving stem. Remove and replace blossom end with a clove. Lay pears on sides in large saucepan. In a small bowl, blend Marsala wine with cinnamon and brown sugar. Pour over pears. Cover and gently poach pears about 45 minutes or until they are tender. Turn over several times during poaching.

When done, lift out onto a serving platter or a 2 quart glass dish. Add cinnamon candies to saucepan and cook liquid another 5 minutes or until it becomes thick and syrupy and all candy is dissolved. Before serving, pour liquid over and around pears. Top each pear with a dollop of raspberry preserves and a mint leaf.

SERVES: 10 ===== **NUTRITIONAL INFORMATION PER SERVING** =====

Calories	210	Total Fat	1 g	Cholesterol	0 mg
Calories from Fat	3%	Saturated Fat	< 1 g	Sodium	8 mg

PEACH TART

As pretty as it is tasty, you can't go wrong serving this luscious tart.

non-stick cooking spray
1 single crust pie dough, unbaked
   (Traditional Crust recipe works well.
   See page 50.)
1 cup nonfat vanilla yogurt
2 tablespoons flour
2 egg whites

3/4 cup sugar, divided
1 teaspoon vanilla extract
4 large peaches, peeled and sliced or
   1 15-ounce can, drained and sliced
1 1/2 teaspoons cornstarch
1/2 cup water
1 tablespoon butter

Preheat oven to 400° F. Spray a 9-inch removable-bottom tart pan or pie pan with non-stick cooking spray. Roll dough to fit pan bringing it up on the sides. Bake for 10 minutes. Remove from oven.

Reduce heat to 350° F. Beat yogurt with flour, egg whites, 1/4 cup sugar and vanilla extract. Pour into prebaked pie crust and bake until filling is set, about 20 minutes. Cool slightly.

Place peaches in a circle around top of pie, leaving an empty circle in the center. In a medium-sized pan, blend remaining sugar with cornstarch and water. Heat, while using a whisk to make a smooth sauce. Mix in butter to finish sauce. Pour over peaches. Allow to cool before slicing.

SERVES: 8	NUTRITIONAL INFORMATION PER SERVING*		
Calories	245	Total Fat	3 g	Cholesterol	3 mg
Calories from Fat	14%	Saturated Fat	1 g	Sodium	94 mg

Nutritional information is based on recipe made with Traditional Crust.

PUMPKIN PIE

This mildly-spiced pie uses a caramelizing technique for added flavor.

1 1/2 cups canned pumpkin purée
2 eggs
3/4 cup brown sugar, packed
1 6-ounce can evaporated skim milk
1/4 teaspoon ginger
1/8 teaspoon nutmeg
1 teaspoon cinnamon

1/2 teaspoon salt
1/4 cup nonfat milk
2 tablespoons boiling water
1 single crust pie shell, unbaked
   (Traditional Crust works well.
   See page 50.)

Preheat oven to 425° F. Pour pumpkin purée into a large non-stick sauce pan. Set stove to a medium-high heat and cook purée until it is dried out and begins to caramelize. Remove from heat and allow to cool.

In a medium-sized bowl, blend eggs with sugar, evaporated milk, spices, salt and milk. Carefully add boiling water, a little at a time. Stir to blend. Beat egg mixture into pumpkin mixture loosening the little flecks and bits of caramelized pumpkin. Pour into crust.

Bake 15 minutes to cook crust before reducing heat to 300° F. Bake an additional 25 minutes or until the middle is almost set.

SERVES: 8 ═══ NUTRITIONAL INFORMATION PER SERVING* ═══

Calories	173	Total Fat	2 g	Cholesterol	54 mg
Calories from Fat	11%	Saturated Fat	1 g	Sodium	192 mg

* Nutritional information is based on recipe made with Traditional Crust.

BLUEBERRY CHEESECAKE PIE

A gorgeous presentation when served in a Meringue Crust.

1/4 cup cornstarch
1 cup apple juice
1/4 cup sugar
1 cup nonfat blueberry yogurt

2 cups fresh blueberries
1 single crust pie shell, baked
 (Meringue Crust works well.
 See page 48.)

In a medium-sized saucepan, combine cornstarch with apple juice to make a thick paste. Blend in sugar. Heat on stove, whisking to make a smooth sauce. Cool slightly and fold in yogurt.

Pour filling into prepared pie shell. Top with blueberries. Chill in refrigerator for 4 hours or until pie is set.

SERVES: 8		NUTRITIONAL INFORMATION PER SERVING*			
Calories	151	Total Fat	< 1 g	Cholesterol	< 1 mg
Calories from Fat	3%	Saturated Fat	< 1 g	Sodium	167 mg

* Nutritional information is based on recipe made with Meringue Crust.

ELBERTA PEACH MELBA

🕐 *A simple, yet elegant dessert.*

1 12-ounce package frozen
 raspberries, defrosted
4 peach halves, canned or fresh

2 pints vanilla or coffee fat-free
 ice cream

In a blender, purée berries until smooth. Place each peach half in a small bowl. Top with a scoop of ice cream and drizzle with raspberry purée.

SERVES: 4		NUTRITIONAL INFORMATION PER SERVING			
Calories	110	Total Fat	< 1 g	Cholesterol	0 mg
Calories from Fat	4%	Saturated Fat	< 1 g	Sodium	55 mg

CHERRY CLAFOUTI

🕐 *A nice change from pies and cobblers, clafouti is a big crisp pancake sitting atop cherries or any other berry.*

non-stick cooking spray
1 16-ounce can cherries, drained
1/2 cup all-purpose flour
1/2 teaspoon salt
1/4 cup sugar
1/2 teaspoon lemon zest

1/4 teaspoon cinnamon
1/2 cup nonfat milk
1 cup nonfat yogurt
1 egg
1 teaspoon vanilla extract

Preheat oven to 425° F. Spray a 9-inch round baking pan with non-stick cooking spray. Spread canned cherries on the bottom of the baking pan. In a medium-sized mixing bowl, blend flour with salt, sugar, lemon zest and cinnamon. In a small bowl, beat milk, yogurt, egg and vanilla extract. Beat wet ingredients into dry ingredients until well-blended. Smooth batter onto the top of the cherries. Bake 25 minutes or until golden brown.

SERVES: 8 ══════ **NUTRITIONAL INFORMATION PER SERVING** ══════

Calories	118	Total Fat	2 g	Cholesterol	27 mg
Calories from Fat	18%	Saturated Fat	< 1 g	Sodium	162 mg

CHOCOLATE SUNDAE PIE

Everybody's favorite treat!

1 quart fat-free vanilla or
  cherry ice cream
1 single crust pie shell, baked (Crunchy
  Cereal Crust works well. See page 49.)

3 tablespoons cocoa powder
1/2 cup brown sugar
3/4 cup water, divided
2 tablespoons arrowroot

Soften ice cream and scoop into baked pie shell. Freeze. In a medium-sized saucepan over a medium heat, whisk together cocoa, sugar and 1/2 cup water. In a separate bowl, blend remaining water with arrowroot.

Remove saucepan from heat and whisk in arrowroot mixture. Return to heat and whisk until thickened. Be cautious, chocolate burns! To serve, cut pie into 8 wedges. Pour hot fudge over each serving.

SERVES: 8 ══════ **NUTRITIONAL INFORMATION PER SERVING*** ══════

| Calories | 237 | Total Fat | 3 g | Cholesterol | 6 mg |
| Calories from Fat | 20% | Saturated Fat | 1 g | Sodium | 290 mg |

*Nutritional information is based on recipe made with Crunchy Cereal Crust

FRUIT PIZZA

Colorful and delicious, a great party dessert.

non-stick cooking spray
1 single crust pie shell, unbaked
   (Traditional Crust works well.
   See page 50.)
1 cup sugar
1/4 teaspoon salt
2 tablespoons cornstarch
1 cup orange juice
1/4 cup lemon juice

2/3 cup water
1/2 teaspoon orange zest
1/2 teaspoon lemon zest
1 pint fresh strawberries, stemmed
   and halved (reserve 7)
3 fresh peaches, peeled and sliced
1 1/2 cups seedless green grapes
1 medium banana, sliced
1 cup light whipped topping

Preheat oven to 475° F. Spray a 14-inch round pizza pan with non-stick cooking spray. Roll dough to fit pizza pan (or use a baking sheet). Flute edges of dough. Prick bottom and bake 8 to 10 minutes. Cool.

Combine sugar, salt and cornstarch in a small pan. Gradually add orange juice, lemon juice and water. Cook over medium heat, stirring constantly until mixture thickens and boils for 1 minute. Remove from heat and stir in orange and lemon zests. Cool.

Arrange strawberry halves around edge of pastry shell. Place peaches in a circle next to strawberries. Mound grapes in a circle next to the peaches. Then arrange a circle of overlapping banana slices. Place whole berries in the center. Spoon sauce over the fruit. To serve, garnish with whipped topping and remaining sauce.

SERVES: 12 ══════════ NUTRITIONAL INFORMATION PER SERVING ══════

Calories	243	Total Fat	3 g	Cholesterol	< 1 mg
Calories from Fat	11%	Saturated Fat	< 1 g	Sodium	99 mg

* Nutritional information is based on recipe made with Traditional Crust.

PEACH COBBLER

Making cobbler with peaches is easy. Use fresh fruit when in season and canned when not.

non-stick cooking spray
1 28-ounce can peaches, drained and
   sliced (or 4 pounds fresh peaches,
   pitted, peeled, and sliced)
2/3 cup plus 1 tablespoon
   sugar, divided
juice of 1 lemon
1 cup all-purpose flour

1 teaspoon baking powder
1/4 teaspoon salt
1/4 teaspoon allspice
1 teaspoon cinnamon
1/4 cup vegetable oil
1/2 teaspoon vanilla extract
1/2 cup low-fat milk

Preheat oven to 400 ° F. Spray a 2-quart baking pan with non-stick cooking spray.

Spread the peaches in the baking pan. Sprinkle them evenly with lemon juice and with 1/3 cup of sugar.

In a medium-sized bowl, combine flour with the baking powder, salt, allspice and cinnamon. In a separate bowl, blend the oil with 1/3 cup sugar and vanilla extract. Alternately add flour mixture and milk to the oil mixture. Beat until smooth. Spread over the peaches. Sprinkle top with 1 tablespoon sugar. Bake 40 minutes or until topping is well-browned and firm in the center. Serve warm.

SERVES: 8 ═══════════ **NUTRITIONAL INFORMATION PER SERVING** ═══════

Calories	178	Total Fat	4 g	Cholesterol	< 1 mg
Calories from Fat	18%	Saturated Fat	< 1 g	Sodium	121 mg

BAKED APPLES

🕐 *As glorious as a piece of pie but without the crust. A wonderful aroma as it bakes.*

6 large baking apples, such as Rome,
   Jonathan or Granny Smith
non-stick cooking spray
3/4 cup raisins
1/2 cup brown sugar, packed
1 tablespoon light margarine

1/2 teaspoon ground cinnamon
1/4 teaspoon ground nutmeg
1/4 teaspoon ground cloves
1/2 cup water
1 cup nonfat frozen yogurt of fat-free
   ice cream

Core the apples with a wide corer. Make a collar around each apple by cutting a strip of peel from around the top of each apple. Spray a large, microwavable dish with non-stick cooking spray. Place apples in dish. Fill the apples with raisins. In a 1-quart microwave bowl, combine brown sugar, margarine, cinnamon, nutmeg, cloves and water. Cover and microwave on high for 1 minute. Stir. Cook on high for another 30 seconds.

If you are not using a microwave, combine ingredients in a medium-sized saucepan and stir over a high heat until sugar has melted and the mixture is very hot.

Carefully, pour the hot mixture over and around apples. Cover the apples with waxed paper or plastic wrap and microwave on high for 10 to 12 minutes, turning dish every 3 minutes. Baste throughout so that fallen spices can penetrate apples. Apples will be hot and very tender.

In a conventional oven, bake at 350° F for 45 minutes in an oven-safe pan. Remove the apples to individual serving dishes. Serve with nonfat frozen yogurt or fat-free ice cream.

SERVES: 6 ═══════ **NUTRITIONAL INFORMATION PER SERVING** ═══════

Calories	226	Total Fat	2 g	Cholesterol	< 1 mg
Calories from Fat	6%	Saturated Fat	< 1 g	Sodium	51 mg

SWEET POTATO PIE

A fragrant and spicy alternative to pumpkin pie.

3 medium-sized sweet potatoes or yams,
    baked until tender
2 eggs, separated, at room temperature
1 tablespoon light margarine
1/2 cup honey
1/4 teaspoon salt
1/4 teaspoon nutmeg

1 teaspoon baking powder
1/2 cup nonfat milk
1/2 teaspoon orange zest
1 teaspoon brandy or vanilla extract
1 single crust pie shell, baked (Crunchy
    Cereal Crust works well. See page 49.)
3 tablespoons sugar

Preheat oven to 300° F. Peel baked sweet potatoes and put through a food
mill. When cool, blend in egg yolks, margarine, honey, salt, nutmeg, baking
powder, milk, orange zest and brandy. Beat vigorously until the mixture is
smooth. Pour into prepared crust and bake 50 to 55 minutes or until the
middle is almost set.

In a clean, medium-sized bowl, beat egg whites until frothy. Sift in sugar,
1 tablespoon at a time, and beat until stiff peaks form. Spread over sweet
potato mixture, making sure the meringue touches all edges. Return to oven
and bake an additional 15 minutes or until meringue is lightly browned.

SERVES: 8 ═══════════ **NUTRITIONAL INFORMATION PER SERVING*** ══════

Calories	114	Total Fat	2 g	Cholesterol	54 mg
Calories from Fat	18%	Saturated Fat	1 g	Sodium	177 mg

* Nutritional information is based on recipe made with Crunchy Cereal Crust.

APRICOT BAVARIAN PIE

To serve Apricot Bavarian as a custard, omit the crust, divide the delicious filling into 6 sherbet glasses, garnish with almonds and freeze for one hour before serving.

1 6-ounce can evaporated skim milk
1 15-ounce can apricots
2 tablespoons gelatin
1/2 cup sugar

2 teaspoons lemon juice
1 tablespoon slivered almonds, toasted
Graham Cracker Crust (See page 39.)

Place evaporated milk in a medium-sized bowl in the freezer along with beaters. Chill until ice crystals form around edges of bowl. Drain can of apricots into a bowl, reserving 1/3 cup of the juice. Purée apricots in a blender or food processor.

Soak gelatin in the apricot juice in the top of a double boiler with very hot water in the bottom. Melt softened gelatin over the hot water. Remove from heat. Add sugar, lemon juice and apricot purée. Chill until mixture is syrupy.

Remove bowl and beaters from freezer. Whip evaporated milk with remaining sugar until mixture is thick and will hold peaks. Combine with gelatin mixture, beating vigorously as the cold mixture will cause the gelatin to harden. Pour into Graham Cracker Crust and freeze for 1 hour before serving. Garnish with almonds.

SERVES: 6	NUTRITIONAL INFORMATION PER SERVING*				
Calories	123	Total Fat	< 1 g	Cholesterol	< 1 mg
Calories from Fat	6%	Saturated Fat	< 1 g	Sodium	46 mg

Nutritional information is based on recipe made without crust

APPLE STRUDEL

Perfect with a scoop of vanilla nonfat frozen yogurt and hot coffee or tea.

non-stick cooking spray
1 cup raisins, plumped by steaming
  over hot water for 5 minutes
1/3 cup butter
1 1/2 cups sugar
1/2 teaspoon lemon zest

2 teaspoons cinnamon
2 cups fine bread crumbs
2 large baking apples, peeled and diced
8 sheets frozen filo dough, defrosted
  and wrapped in a damp dish towel
2 tablespoons honey

Preheat oven to 400° F. Spray a 17 x 11 x 1-inch jelly-roll pan with non-stick cooking spray. In a small bowl, combine hot raisins with butter. In another small bowl, mix sugar with lemon zest and cinnamon.

Place a clean, damp dish towel on a large working surface. One at a time, spray the 4 sheets of filo with non-stick spray and carefully lay them on top of each other on towel. Keep remaining filo sheets wrapped in damp towel until ready to make second strudel.

In a continuous strip, 4 inches wide and 2 inches in from a long edge of the top filo sheet, spread 1/2 cup bread crumbs, half of the apples, half of the sugar mixture, half of the raisins, and top with another 1/2 cup of the bread crumbs. Fold edges of filo dough over the filling to seal ingredients into the dough. Roll strudel, jelly-roll style, from one narrow end to the other. Place on prepared pan.

Repeat entire procedure for second strudel. Brush both strudels with honey. If desired, score before baking for easier cutting. Bake 20 to 25 minutes or until strudels are browned. Remove from pan while still hot. Cool and cut each strudel into 6 slices.

1 PER SERVING ======== **NUTRITIONAL INFORMATION PER SERVING** ========

Calories	102	Total Fat	2 g	Cholesterol	7 mg
Calories from Fat	18%	Saturated Fat	1 g	Sodium	50 mg

Cookies & Bars

Whether served in lunch boxes or on dessert
plates, the following treats are delicious
adaptations of everyone's favorite sweets.

BLONDIES

A delicious bar with a butterscotch flavor.

non-stick cooking spray
2 cups all-purpose flour
2 teaspoons baking powder
1/4 teaspoon salt
1/4 cup butter or margarine
1/4 cup corn syrup

1 1/2 cups brown sugar
1 egg
1 teaspoon vanilla extract
1/4 cup water
1 tablespoon walnuts, toasted
  and chopped

Preheat oven to 350° F. Spray a 9-inch baking pan with non-stick cooking spray.

In a large bowl, combine flour, baking powder and salt. In a medium-sized mixing bowl, blend butter, corn syrup, sugar, egg, vanilla extract and water. Stir into dry ingredients. Spread mixture into pan, smoothing into all the corners with a wetted spatula. Sprinkle with walnuts.

Bake 30 to 35 minutes. While still warm, cut into 24 bars.

1 PER SERVING ══════ **NUTRITIONAL INFORMATION PER SERVING*** ══════

| Calories | 121 | Total Fat | 2 g | Cholesterol | 14 mg |
| Calories from Fat | 17% | Saturated Fat | 1 g | Sodium | 78 mg |

* Nutritional information based on recipe made with butter.

APPLESAUCE COOKIES

🍪 *Honey is the magic in this chewy, tasty cookie.*

non-stick cooking spray
1 cup oatmeal
2 cups all-purpose flour
1/2 teaspoon baking soda
1/2 teaspoon baking powder
1 1/2 teaspoons cinnamon
1/2 cup honey

1/3 cup corn syrup
2 tablespoons margarine
3/4 cup applesauce
1 egg
1 teaspoon vanilla extract
3/4 cup raisins, plumped by
    steaming over hot water 5 minutes

Preheat oven to 350° F. Spray 2 cookie sheets with non-stick cooking spray.

In a large bowl, combine oatmeal, flour, baking soda, baking powder and cinnamon. In a medium-sized saucepan, heat honey to melt. Stir in corn syrup, margarine, applesauce, egg, vanilla extract and raisins. Add honey mixture to dry ingredients and blend well.

Drop onto cookie sheets by rounded teaspoonfuls. Recipe makes 36 cookies. Bake 10 to 12 minutes. Remove from cookie sheets and cool on wire racks. Store in an air-tight container.

1 PER SERVING ══════ **NUTRITIONAL INFORMATION PER SERVING** ══════

Calories	61	Total Fat	1 g	Cholesterol	6 mg
Calories from Fat	6%	Saturated Fat	< 1 g	Sodium	45 mg

BAKE WHILE YOU SLEEP COOKIES

For those short on time, you can bake while you sleep.

2 egg whites, at room temperature	2/3 cup sugar
1/4 teaspoon cream of tartar	1/2 cup low-fat chocolate morsels
1/8 teaspoon salt	1 teaspoon vanilla extract

Preheat oven to 350° F. Cover a cookie sheet with aluminum foil. In a medium-sized bowl, whip egg whites with cream of tartar and salt until the mixture is foamy. Sift sugar, 2 tablespoons at a time, into egg whites, continuing to whip on high speed until stiff peaks form. Make sure all sugar has been incorporated into the egg whites. (You can tell this by pinching a bit of the whipped egg white between your fingers. If sugar has been incorporated, you will feel no grains.) Fold in chocolate morsels and vanilla extract.

Drop by teaspoonfuls onto aluminum foil. Recipe makes 24 cookies. Put cookies in the oven and turn the oven off, closing the door. Do not open for 8 hours.

1 PER SERVING ═══════ **NUTRITIONAL INFORMATION PER SERVING** ═══════

Calories	34	Total Fat	1 g	Cholesterol	0 mg
Calories from Fat	20%	Saturated Fat	< 1 g	Sodium	29 mg

ALMOND DIPPING COOKIES

Crisp and crunchy, this is the perfect dipping cookie.

non-stick cooking spray
2 cups all-purpose flour
1 teaspoon baking soda
1 teaspoon baking powder
1/2 cup sugar
2 tablespoons butter

2 tablespoons corn syrup
3 egg whites, whipped with a fork
1 teaspoon almond extract
2 tablespoons slivered
   almonds, chopped

Preheat oven to 350° F. Spray a cookie sheet with non-stick cooking spray. In a large bowl, combine flour, baking soda, baking powder and sugar. In a small bowl, cream butter with corn syrup. With 2 knives or a pastry cutter, cut the butter mixture into the flour mixture, creating a texture of small-sized granules. Blend in egg whites, almond extract and almonds. Divide dough into 2 pieces.

Shape each piece into a 10-inch log and place on cookie sheet 2 inches apart. Bake 25 minutes or until lightly browned. Remove from pan onto cooling rack. Do not turn off oven. Cool for 5 minutes. Using a very sharp knife, slice logs into 12 cookies each, about 3/4-inch wide. Place cookies back onto cookie sheet and bake another 15 to 18 minutes or until cookies are very dry. Cool and enjoy. Store in an air-tight container.

1 PER SERVING ═══════ **NUTRITIONAL INFORMATION PER SERVING** ═══════

Calories	74	Total Fat	1 g	Cholesterol	3 mg
Calories from Fat	17%	Saturated Fat	1 g	Sodium	66 mg

BROWN SUGAR SANDIES

A deceptively plain-looking cookie that delivers on taste. To dress up these cookies, cut into shapes or glaze with sugar-milk icing (see page 30).

non-stick cooking spray
1 1/2 cups brown sugar
1/2 cup light margarine
4 egg whites
1/4 cup apple juice

2 1/2 cups all-purpose flour
1 teaspoon baking soda
1 teaspoon baking powder
1 teaspoon allspice
1 tablespoon cinnamon

Preheat oven to 375 ° F. Spray a cookie sheet with non-stick cooking spray. In a large bowl, use an electric mixer to cream brown sugar with margarine, egg whites, and apple juice. In a medium-sized bowl, combine flour, baking soda, baking powder, allspice and cinnamon.

Mix the dry ingredients into the brown sugar mixture, a little at a time. The mixture will be very firm. Place dough on a floured board and roll out to about 1/2 inch thick. Cut into rounds or other shapes with a floured cookie cutter. Recipe makes 36 cookies. Place onto prepared cookie sheet and bake 10 to 12 minutes or until edges are lightly browned.

1 PER SERVING ══════ **NUTRITIONAL INFORMATION PER SERVING** ══════

Calories	60	Total Fat	1 g	Cholesterol	0 mg
Calories from Fat	20%	Saturated Fat	< 1 g	Sodium	68 mg

CHOCOLATE BISCOTTI

A wonderful chocolate dipping cookie. Great with milk, coffee or hot cocoa.

non-stick cooking spray
2 cups all-purpose flour
1 teaspoon baking soda
1 teaspoon baking powder
1/2 cup sugar
2 tablespoons cocoa

2 tablespoons butter
2 tablespoons corn syrup
3 egg whites, whipped with a fork
2 tablespoons almonds,
    chopped and slivered

Preheat oven to 350° F. Spray a cookie sheet with non-stick cooking spray. In a large bowl, combine flour, baking soda, baking powder, sugar and cocoa. In a small bowl, cream butter and corn syrup. With 2 knives or a pastry cutter, cut the butter mixture into the flour mixture, creating a texture of small-sized granules. Blend in egg whites, almond extract and almonds. Divide into 2 pieces.

Shape each piece into a 10-inch log and place on cookie sheet 2 inches apart. Bake 25 minutes or until lightly browned. Remove from cookie sheet onto cooling rack. Do not turn off oven. Cool for 5 minutes. Using a very sharp knife, slice logs into 12 cookies each, about 3/4-inch wide. Place cookies back onto cookie sheet and bake another 15 to 18 minutes or until cookies are very dry. Cool and enjoy. Store in an air-tight container.

1 PER SERVING ═══ **NUTRITIONAL INFORMATION PER SERVING** ═══

Calories	73	Total Fat	1 g	Cholesterol	3 mg
Calories from Fat	17%	Saturated Fat	1 g	Sodium	66 mg

FRUIT BARS

A hearty treat with a sweet and fruity punch.

non-stick cooking spray
3/4 cup boiling water
1 cup dried mixed fruit (available
    packaged in produce department)
1/4 cup banana chips
1 3/4 cups oatmeal
2 cups all-purpose flour
1/2 teaspoon baking soda

1/2 teaspoon cream of tartar
1 egg
2 tablespoons butter or margarine,
    melted
1 cup sugar
1/2 cup apple juice
1 teaspoon almond extract
1 teaspoon vanilla extract

Preheat oven to 350° F. Spray a 9-inch baking pan with non-stick cooking spray.

In a small bowl, combine boiling water, dried fruit and banana chips. Set aside to soak.

In a large bowl, blend oatmeal, flour, baking soda, and cream of tartar. In a small bowl, blend egg with butter, sugar, apple juice, almond extract and vanilla extract. Mix into dry ingredients. Use a wetted spoon to spread half of the batter into the prepared pan.

In a blender, purée dried fruit and water. Spread purée on top of batter. Cover with remaining batter. Bake 30 to 35 minutes or until nicely browned. Cool and cut into 24 pieces.

1 PER SERVING		NUTRITIONAL INFORMATION PER SERVING*			
Calories	123	Total Fat	2 g	Cholesterol	11 mg
Calories from Fat	13%	Saturated Fat	1 g	Sodium	41 mg

Nutritional information based on recipe made with butter.

CHOCOLATE CHIP COOKIES

🕐 *Everybody's favorite.*

non-stick cooking spray
1 1/4 cups all-purpose flour
1/3 cup sugar
3/4 teaspoon baking soda
1/3 cup corn syrup

2 tablespoons butter
2 tablespoons honey
1 teaspoon vanilla extract
2 egg whites, whipped with a fork
6 tablespoons low-fat chocolate morsels

Preheat oven to 350° F. Spray 2 cookie sheets with non-stick cooking spray. In a large bowl, combine flour, sugar and baking soda. In a small bowl, cream corn syrup with butter, honey, vanilla extract and egg whites. Cream until very smooth. Blend creamed ingredients into dry ones. Blend in chocolate morsels. The dough will be sticky.

Drop by tablespoonfuls onto prepared cookie sheets, leaving 2 inches between each cookie. Recipe makes 24 cookies. Bake 12 to 15 minutes or until cookies are browned. Cool slightly, then remove from cookie sheet to a cooling rack. Cool completely and store in an air-tight container.

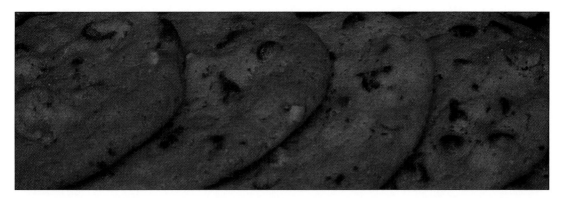

1 PER SERVING ═══════ · **NUTRITIONAL INFORMATION PER SERVING** ═══════

Calories	69	Total Fat	1 g	Cholesterol	3 mg
Calories from Fat	20%	Saturated Fat	1 g	Sodium	43 mg

GINGERSNAPS

Molasses and ginger come together in a perfect tea-time snack.

non-stick cooking spray
1/4 cup butter or margarine
1/2 cup light molasses
1/2 cup sugar
1 tablespoon vinegar

2 cups all-purpose flour
1 teaspoon cinnamon
1 teaspoon finely grated fresh ginger
 (or 1/2 teaspoon ground)
1 1/2 teaspoons baking soda

In a small saucepan, heat butter, molasses, sugar and vinegar. Bring to a boil and then lower heat, simmering ingredients for 3 minutes. Remove from heat and set aside to cool.

In a large bowl, sift flour with cinnamon, ginger and baking soda.

Use an electric beater to blend molasses mixture, about a third at a time, into dry ingredients. Mix until very smooth. Shape into a log, 12 inches long and 2 inches in diameter. Wrap with plastic and chill until cold.

To make cookies, preheat oven to 375° F. Spray 2 cookie sheets with non-stick cooking spray. Slice cookies into very thin slices, 1/4 inch thick. Place 1 1/2 inches apart on prepared cookie sheets. Recipe makes 48 cookies. Bake 7 minutes or until rich brown. Remove from cookie sheets immediately. Place on a cooling rack. Cool completely and store in an air-tight container.

1 PER SERVING ═══ **NUTRITIONAL INFORMATION PER SERVING*** ═══

| Calories | 43 | Total Fat | 1 g | Cholesterol | 3 mg |
| Calories from Fat | 20% | Saturated Fat | 1 g | Sodium | 36 mg |

* Nutritional information based on recipe made with butter.

CHOCOLATE FUDGE BROWNIES

A dense and delicious chocolate brownie with a built-in crunch.

non-stick cooking spray
1 cup sugar
1 cup cake flour, sifted
1/4 teaspoon salt
1/4 cup cocoa
1/4 cup applesauce

1 teaspoon vanilla extract
3 tablespoons butter, softened
1/2 cup buttermilk
1 egg
2 egg whites, whipped with a fork
1 cup crisp rice cereal

Preheat oven to 350° F. Spray a 9-inch baking pan with non-stick cooking spray. In a large bowl, combine sugar, cake flour, salt and cocoa. In a small bowl, blend applesauce, vanilla extract, butter, buttermilk, egg and egg whites. Stir wet ingredients into dry ingredients, stirring until batter is well-blended. Fold in cereal.

Pour into prepared pan. Bake 25 to 30 minutes or until center is firm to the touch. Remove from oven, cool slightly, and cut into 16 brownies.

1 PER SERVING ════ **NUTRITIONAL INFORMATION PER SERVING** ════

Calories	113	Total Fat	2 g	Cholesterol	19 mg
Calories from Fat	20%	Saturated Fat	1 g	Sodium	92 mg

RUM RAISIN BARS

A perfect treat with coffee or tea.

non-stick cooking spray
1 cup raisins
2/3 cup coffee, hot and strong
2 tablespoons dark rum or
   1 teaspoon rum extract
1/2 teaspoon cinnamon
1/3 cup vegetable oil
1/3 cup corn syrup
1 cup sugar
2 eggs

1 1/2 cups all-purpose flour, sifted
1/2 teaspoon baking powder
1/2 teaspoon baking soda
1/4 teaspoon salt

Glaze:
1/2 cup confectioners sugar, sifted
1 to 2 teaspoons coffee,
   brewed and cooled

Preheat oven to 350° F. Spray an 11 x 13-inch jelly-roll pan with non-stick cooking spray. In a small bowl, combine raisins, coffee, rum and cinnamon. In a large bowl, cream vegetable oil with corn syrup, sugar and eggs. In a medium-sized bowl, blend flour with baking powder, baking soda and salt. Stir raisin mixture into creamed ingredients. Add dry ingredients and mix well. Press mixture into prepared pan. Bake 20 to 30 minutes.

To make glaze, mix confectioners sugar with just enough coffee to make mixture easily spreadable. Glaze tops of hot bars. To serve, cut into 24 bars.

1 PER SERVING ════════ **NUTRITIONAL INFORMATION PER SERVING** ════════

Calories	132	Total Fat	4 g	Cholesterol	1 mg
Calories from Fat	20%	Saturated Fat	< 1 g	Sodium	34 mg

Rum Raisin Bars make a nice snack with a scoop of fat-free ice cream.

GRANOLA BARS

🕐 *A delicious, tender bar that's quick and easy to make.*

non-stick cooking spray
1/4 cup honey
1 egg, beaten

1 tablespoon butter
2 cups fat-free granola with fruit pieces

Preheat oven to 300° F. Spray an 8-inch square pan with non-stick cooking spray. In a medium-sized bowl, blend honey, egg and butter. Fold in granola. Press into prepared pan. Bake 20 minutes or until lightly browned. Cool and cut into 12 bars. Store in an air-tight container.

1 PER SERVING		NUTRITIONAL INFORMATION PER SERVING			
Calories	82	Total Fat	2 g	Cholesterol	19 mg
Calories from Fat	16%	Saturated Fat	< 1 g	Sodium	9 mg

KONA HERMITS

A perfect combination of Hawaii's finest flavors.

non-stick cooking spray
2 tablespoons butter, softened
1/3 cup corn syrup
1 cup brown sugar, packed
1 egg
1/4 cup apple juice
1 cup Kona coffee, cold
1 3/4 cups all-purpose flour

1/2 teaspoon baking soda
1/2 teaspoon salt
1/2 teaspoon nutmeg
1/2 teaspoon cinnamon
1 1/4 cups raisins
2 tablespoons Macadamia
  nuts, chopped

In a small bowl, cream butter with corn syrup, brown sugar, egg, apple juice and coffee. In a medium-sized bowl, blend flour with baking soda, salt and spices. Stir the dry mixture into the creamed mixture. Add raisins and nuts. Chill for at least 4 hours.

Preheat oven to 400° F. Spray a cookie sheet with non-stick cooking spray.

Drop batter by teaspoonfuls onto cookie sheet, leaving 2 inches between each cookie. Recipe makes 48 cookies. Bake 8 to 10 minutes or until cookies are lightly browned.

1 PER SERVING		NUTRITIONAL INFORMATION PER SERVING			
Calories	60	Total Fat	1 g	Cholesterol	6 mg
Calories from Fat	12%	Saturated Fat	< 1 g	Sodium	41 mg

LEMON BARS

A tangy lemon filling and a delicious crust.

non-stick cooking spray
1 cup flour
2 tablespoons butter or margarine
1/3 cup corn syrup
1/4 cup confectioners sugar
2 eggs

1 cup granulated sugar
1/2 teaspoon baking powder
1/4 teaspoon salt
2 tablespoons freshly squeezed
   lemon juice

Preheat oven to 350° F. Spray an 8-inch square baking pan with non-stick cooking spray. In a medium-sized bowl, mix flour with butter, corn syrup and confectioners sugar. Press into prepared pan. Bake 20 minutes or until browned.

In a separate bowl, beat eggs, sugar, baking powder, salt and lemon juice until mixture is light and fluffy. Pour onto hot crust. Bake 25 minutes until the cake springs back when touched in the center. Cool, sprinkle with a little confectioners sugar and cut into 12 squares.

1 PER SERVING		NUTRITIONAL INFORMATION PER SERVING*			
Calories	108	Total Fat	2 g	Cholesterol	27 mg
Calories from Fat	15%	Saturated Fat	1 g	Sodium	63 mg

* Nutritional information based on recipe made with butter.

OATMEAL CHUNK COOKIES

🕐 *Scrumptious oatmeal and a chunk of chocolate make for a savory and satisfying cookie.*

non-stick cooking spray
1 cup oatmeal, uncooked
1 cup all-purpose flour
1/4 cup sugar
2 tablespoons baking powder
1 teaspoon baking soda
1/2 cup nonfat chocolate syrup

2 eggs
1/4 cup water
1 teaspoon vanilla extract
1/4 cup raisins, plumped for five
    minutes over boiling water
1/3 cup chocolate chunks, 36 chunks

Preheat oven to 325° F. Spray 2 cookie sheets with non-stick cooking spray. In a large bowl, combine oatmeal, flour, sugar, baking powder and baking soda. In a small bowl, blend chocolate syrup with eggs, water and vanilla extract. Blend wet ingredients into dry ingredients. Fold in raisins.

Drop cookies by undersized tablespoonfuls onto prepared cookie sheets. Recipe makes 36 cookies. Press a chocolate chunk into the top of each. Bake 15 to 18 minutes or until cookies are browned. Cool slightly, then remove from cookie sheet to a cooling rack. Cool completely and store in an air-tight container.

1 PER SERVING ══════ **NUTRITIONAL INFORMATION PER SERVING** ══════

Calories	51	Total Fat	1 g	Cholesterol	12 mg
Calories from Fat	19%	Saturated Fat	< 1 g	Sodium	61 mg

OATMEAL NUT SQUARES

Hearty, nutritious and delicious.

non-stick cooking spray
1 1/3 cups oatmeal
2 small bananas, mashed
1/4 cup water
1/2 cup sugar
2 eggs

2 teaspoons vanilla extract
1 tablespoon cornstarch
1/2 cup all-purpose flour
1 teaspoon baking powder
1/2 cup chopped walnuts

Preheat oven to 325° F. Spray an 8-inch square baking pan with non-stick cooking spray. In a medium-sized bowl, combine oatmeal, banana and water and set aside to soften. In a separate bowl, cream sugar with eggs and add to banana mixture. Mix in vanilla extract. In a small bowl, blend cornstarch, flour, baking powder and walnuts. Blend into banana mixture. Spread batter into prepared pan. Bake 20 to 25 minutes or until center is firm. Cool and cut into 16 bars.

1 PER SERVING		NUTRITIONAL INFORMATION PER SERVING			
Calories	112	Total Fat	2 g	Cholesterol	26 mg
Calories from Fat	18%	Saturated Fat	1 g	Sodium	8 mg

NO BAKE COOKIES I

🕐 *For another great No Bake Cookie recipe, see page 184.*

waxed paper
1/2 cup low-fat creamy peanut butter
1/2 cup honey

1/2 cup nonfat dry milk
2 1/2 cups unsweetened cereal flakes,
   coarsely crushed

In a saucepan, heat peanut butter and honey. Stir well over low heat. Mix in dry milk. Stir in cereal. Drop by heaping teaspoonfuls onto waxed paper. Recipe makes 48 cookies. Cool in refrigerator until ready to serve.

1 PER SERVING		NUTRITIONAL INFORMATION PER SERVING			
Calories	37	Total Fat	< 1 g	Cholesterol	71 mg
Calories from Fat	20%	Saturated Fat	< 1 g	Sodium	42 mg

PUMPKIN BARS

A low-calorie, low-fat, mildly spicy bar

non-stick cooking spray
1 16-ounce can pumpkin purée
1/2 cup maple syrup
1/2 cup corn syrup
1 egg
2 egg whites, whipped with a fork

1 teaspoon vanilla extract
2 1/4 cups all-purpose flour
1 teaspoon baking soda
1 teaspoon cinnamon
1/2 teaspoon allspice

Preheat oven to 350° F. Spray a 9-inch baking pan with non-stick cooking spray. In a large bowl, blend pumpkin with maple syrup, corn syrup, egg, egg whites and vanilla extract. In a medium-sized bowl, combine flour,

baking soda, cinnamon and allspice. Fold dry ingredients into pumpkin mixture until just blended. Spread into prepared pan. Bake 50 to 55 minutes or until top is browned. Cool and cut into 24 bars.

1 PER SERVING ═══════ **NUTRITIONAL INFORMATION PER SERVING** ═══════

Calories	38	Total Fat	< 1 g	Cholesterol	9 mg
Calories from Fat	9%	Saturated Fat	< 1 g	Sodium	42 mg

SNICKERDOODLES

🕐 *A delicious and crisp little cookie*

non-stick cooking spray
2 3/4 cups all-purpose flour, sifted
1/4 teaspoon salt
1 teaspoon baking soda
2 teaspoons cream of tartar
1/4 cup butter or margarine, softened
1/4 cup corn syrup

1 1/2 cups sugar
1/4 cup apple juice

Topping
2 tablespoons sugar
2 teaspoons cinnamon

Preheat oven to 350° F. Spray 2 cookie sheets with non-stick cooking spray. In a large bowl, sift flour with salt, baking soda and cream of tartar. In a small bowl, cream butter until light and gradually add corn syrup, sugar and apple juice, creaming until fluffy. Add creamed ingredients to dry ingredients and beat until just smooth. Mixture will be sticky.

Make topping in a small bowl by blending sugar and cinnamon.

Shape batter into 1-inch balls and roll in cinnamon sugar. Arrange 2 inches apart on prepared cookie sheets. Recipe makes 72 small cookies. Bake 18 to 20 minutes or until lightly browned. Cool slightly, then remove from pan to cooling rack. Cool completely and store in an air-tight container.

---

1 PER SERVING ═══ **NUTRITIONAL INFORMATION PER SERVING** ═══

Calories	39	Total Fat	< 1 g	Cholesterol	1 mg
Calories from Fat	20%	Saturated Fat	< 1 g	Sodium	230 mg

* Nutritional information based on recipe made with butter.

Coffeecakes & Muffins

For breakfast, dessert or snack time, coffeecakes and muffins are sweet and satisfying treats. For a moist and fluffy texture, keep the stirring or beating of ingredients to a minimum.

Dress up Maple Sugar Loaf with nonfat topping and berries.

MAPLE SUGAR LOAF

🕐 *Simply scrumptious and so easy to make.*

non-stick cooking spray
2 cups all-purpose flour
2 teaspoons baking powder
1/2 teaspoon baking soda
1 teaspoon salt
1 cup sugar
1/2 cup 1% buttermilk
1/2 cup nonfat sour cream

2 eggs
2 tablespoons vegetable oil
2 tablespoons pure maple syrup
1/2 teaspoon vanilla extract
3 tablespoons brown sugar
2 tablespoons walnuts,
  chopped and toasted
1/2 teaspoon cinnamon

Preheat oven to 350° F. Spray a 9-inch loaf pan with non-stick cooking spray.

In a large bowl, combine flour, baking powder, baking soda, salt and sugar. In a small bowl, blend buttermilk, sour cream, eggs, oil, maple syrup and vanilla extract. Mix wet ingredients into dry ingredients until just blended.

Pour into prepared pan. In a small bowl, combine brown sugar with nuts and cinnamon. Sprinkle over cake. Bake 50 to 60 minutes or until toothpick inserted in center of cake comes out clean. Cool in pan for 10 minutes. Gently loosen sides of loaf and turn out onto wire rack to cool completely.

SERVES: 12 ══ **NUTRITIONAL INFORMATION PER SERVING** ══

| Calories | 157 | Total Fat | 3 g | Cholesterol | 27 mg |
| Calories from Fat | 19% | Saturated Fat | 1 g | Sodium | 233 mg |

APPLE CARROT MUFFINS

Experiment with this recipe by substituting apples with bananas or peaches.

non-stick cooking spray
2 cups all-purpose flour
1 teaspoon baking powder
1/2 teaspoon baking soda
1/2 teaspoon salt
1/2 cup sugar

1/2 cup 1% buttermilk
2 eggs
1 teaspoon vanilla extract
1 tablespoon vegetable oil
1 cup peeled and chopped apples
1 1/2 cups peeled and shredded carrots

Preheat oven to 400° F. Spray 12 muffin tins with non-stick cooking spray.

In a large bowl, combine flour, baking powder, baking soda, salt and sugar. In a small bowl, mix buttermilk, eggs, vanilla extract and oil. Mix wet ingredients into dry ingredients until just blended. Fold in apples and carrots. Let mixture sit for 5 minutes to blend.

Divide batter among muffin cups, filling each about 3/4 full. Bake 20 minutes or until golden brown. Remove from pans and serve immediately or cool on racks and store in an air-tight container.

SERVES: 12	NUTRITIONAL INFORMATION PER SERVING		
Calories	189	Total Fat	2 g	Cholesterol	18 mg
Calories from Fat	11%	Saturated Fat	< 1 g	Sodium	249 mg

SUNSHINE MUFFINS

🕐 *A nutritious muffin that makes a great snack.*

non-stick cooking spray
3 cups all-purpose flour
1 1/2 teaspoons baking powder
1 teaspoon baking soda
1/2 teaspoon salt

3/4 cup brown sugar
1 teaspoon lemon zest
1 tablespoon vegetable oil
1 egg
3/4 cup orange juice

Preheat oven to 400° F. Spray 16 muffin tins with non-stick cooking spray.

In a large bowl, combine flour, baking powder, baking soda, salt and sugar. In a small bowl, blend lemon zest, oil, egg and orange juice. Mix wet ingredients into dry ingredients until just blended.

Divide batter among muffin tins, filling each about 3/4 full. Bake 15 minutes or until muffins are golden brown. Remove from pans and serve immediately or cool on racks and store in an air-tight container.

SERVES: 16 ══════ **NUTRITIONAL INFORMATION PER SERVING** ══════

Calories	137	Total Fat	1 g	Cholesterol	13 mg
Calories from Fat	13%	Saturated Fat	< 1 g	Sodium	133 mg

MAPLE AND NUT MUFFINS

🕐 *The secret to this delicious muffin is real maple syrup.*

non-stick cooking spray
3 cups all-purpose flour
1 teaspoon salt
1/2 teaspoon baking powder
1/2 cup mashed bananas
1/2 cup 1% buttermilk

3/4 cup pure maple syrup
1 teaspoon maple flavoring
2 egg whites
1 tablespoon vegetable oil
1 tablespoon chopped walnuts, toasted

Preheat oven to 400° F. Spray 12 muffin tins with non-stick cooking spray.

In a large bowl, combine flour, salt and baking powder. In a small bowl, blend bananas, buttermilk, maple syrup, maple flavoring, egg whites and vegetable oil. Mix wet ingredients into dry ingredients until just blended. Fold in walnuts.

Divide among muffin tins, filling each about 3/4 full. Bake 15 minutes or until golden brown. Remove from pans and serve immediately or cool on racks and store in an air-tight container.

SERVES: 12	NUTRITIONAL INFORMATION PER SERVING				
Calories	195	Total Fat	2 g	Cholesterol	< 1 mg
Calories from Fat	8%	Saturated Fat	< 1 g	Sodium	218 mg

YOGURT MUFFINS

🕐 *Packed with healthy ingredients and tastes great, too.*

non-stick cooking spray	1 tablespoon vegetable oil
3 cups all-purpose flour	1/4 cup 1% buttermilk
1/2 teaspoon baking soda	1 cup nonfat yogurt
1 teaspoon salt	1/2 cup raisins
1/2 cup brown sugar	2 tablespoons chopped walnuts, toasted
1 egg	

Preheat oven to 400° F. Spray 12 muffin tins with non-stick cooking spray.

In a large bowl, combine flour, baking soda, salt and sugar. In a small bowl, blend egg, oil, buttermilk and yogurt. Mix wet ingredients into dry ingredients until just blended. Fold in raisins and nuts.

Divide among muffin tins, filling each about 3/4 full. Bake 20 minutes or until golden brown. Remove from pans and serve immediately or cool on racks and store in an air-tight container.

SERVES: 12 ══════ **NUTRITIONAL INFORMATION PER SERVING** ══════

Calories	166	Total Fat	3 g	Cholesterol	17 mg
Calories from Fat	14%	Saturated Fat	< 1 g	Sodium	120 mg

RAISIN WHEAT MUFFINS

Dense and chewy, these healthy muffins are full of flavor.

non-stick cooking spray
2 cups all-purpose flour
1 cup whole wheat pastry flour
2 teaspoons baking powder
1/2 teaspoon salt
1 teaspoon cinnamon

1/4 cup sugar
1 cup 1% buttermilk
1 egg
1 tablespoon vegetable oil
2 tablespoons dark molasses
1/2 cup raisins

Preheat oven to 375° F. Spray 12 muffin tins with non-stick cooking spray. In a large bowl, combine white and wheat flours, baking powder, salt, cinnamon and sugar. In a small bowl, blend buttermilk, egg, oil and molasses. Mix wet ingredients into dry ingredients until just blended. Fold in raisins.

Divide among muffin tins, filling each about 3/4 full. Bake 18 to 20 minutes or until golden brown. Remove from pans and serve immediately, or cool on racks and store in an air-tight container.

SERVES: 12	NUTRITIONAL INFORMATION PER SERVING				
Calories	171	Total Fat	2 g	Cholesterol	18 mg
Calories from Fat	10%	Saturated Fat	< 1 g	Sodium	161 mg

APPLE JUICE MUFFINS

🕐 *Almost a meal in a muffin.*

non-stick cooking spray
2 1/2 cups all-purpose flour
2 teaspoons baking powder
1 teaspoon cinnamon
1/4 cup brown sugar
1 egg
1 tablespoon vegetable oil

3/4 cup apple juice concentrate
1 apple, peeled and chopped
1 ripe banana, mashed
1/2 teaspoon vanilla extract
2 tablespoons walnuts,
    chopped and toasted

Preheat oven to 400° F. Spray 16 muffin tins with non-stick cooking spray. In a large bowl, combine flour, baking powder, cinnamon and sugar. In a small bowl, blend egg, oil, apple juice, apple, banana and vanilla extract. Mix wet ingredients into dry ingredients until just blended. Fold in nuts.

Divide among muffin tins, filling each about 3/4 full. Bake 15 minutes or until golden brown. Remove from pans and serve immediately or cool on racks and store in an air-tight container.

SERVES: 16		NUTRITIONAL INFORMATION PER SERVING			
Calories	118	Total Fat	2 g	Cholesterol	13 mg
Calories from Fat	14%	Saturated Fat	< 1 g	Sodium	46 mg

HAWAIIAN MUFFINS

Wonderfully fragrant muffins with a taste of the tropics.

non-stick cooking spray
3 cups all-purpose flour
2 teaspoons baking powder
1 teaspoon salt
1/2 cup sugar
1 egg

1/4 cup 1% buttermilk
1 tablespoon vegetable oil
1 teaspoon vanilla extract
1 15-ounce can crushed pineapple
  with juice
2 tablespoons shredded coconut

Preheat oven to 375° F. Spray 16 muffin tins with non-stick cooking spray.

In a large bowl, combine flour, baking powder, salt and sugar. In a small bowl, blend egg, buttermilk, oil, vanilla extract and pineapple including the juice. Mix wet ingredients into dry ingredients until just blended. Fold in coconut.

Divide among muffin tins, filling each about 3/4 full. Bake 20 minutes or until golden brown. Remove from pans and serve immediately or cool on racks and store in an air-tight container.

SERVES: 16		NUTRITIONAL INFORMATION PER SERVING			
Calories	146	Total Fat	3 g	Cholesterol	13 mg
Calories from Fat	15%	Saturated Fat	1 g	Sodium	183 mg

CINNAMON TOAST COFFEECAKE

🕐 *Served warm from the oven, this coffeecake is a special treat.*

non-stick cooking spray
1 1/4 cups sugar, divided
1 teaspoon salt
2 cups all-purpose flour
1 teaspoon baking soda
1 cup nonfat milk

1 egg
1 tablespoon vegetable oil
1 teaspoon vanilla extract
1 teaspoon cinnamon
2 tablespoons butter, melted

Preheat oven to 325° F. Spray a 9-inch baking pan with non-stick cooking spray.

In a large bowl, combine 1 cup sugar with salt, flour and baking soda. In a medium-sized bowl, blend milk, egg, oil and vanilla extract. Mix wet ingredients into dry ingredients until just blended. Pour into prepared pan.

In a small bowl, blend remaining 1/4 cup sugar with cinnamon. Sprinkle over coffeecake then drizzle butter over cinnamon-sugar mixture. Bake 25 to 30 minutes or until the sugar caramelizes and the cake is nicely browned.

SERVES: 12 ═══════ **NUTRITIONAL INFORMATION PER SERVING** ═══════

Calories	141	Total Fat	3 g	Cholesterol	15 mg
Calories from Fat	18%	Saturated Fat	1 g	Sodium	188 mg

SPOON HANDLE COFFEECAKE

A tried and true recipe that never fails to please.

non-stick cooking spray
3 cups all-purpose flour
1 teaspoon salt
3 tablespoons sugar
1 package dry yeast, 1/4-ounce
1/2 cup very warm water

1 egg
1 cup evaporated skim milk, divided
2 tablespoons butter, melted
1/2 cup brown sugar, packed
3/4 teaspoon cinnamon

Preheat oven to 325° F. Spray two 8-inch round baking pans with non-stick cooking spray.

In a large mixing bowl, combine flour, salt, sugar and yeast. Using an electric mixer, blend in water. Add egg, and 3/4 cup evaporated skim milk. Continue mixing until smooth and satiny, about 5 minutes.

Divide dough into 2 portions. Press into round pans, making sure that dough covers all sides of the pan. Cover and let dough rise in a warm place for 20 minutes.

Mix butter, remaining evaporated skim milk, brown sugar and cinnamon. With a wooden spoon handle, make indentations on the tops of prepared dough. Fill the indentations with brown sugar mixture. Bake 25 minutes or until tops of coffeecakes are lightly browned. This coffeecake freezes and reheats well.

SERVES: 12 ═══════ **NUTRITIONAL INFORMATION PER SERVING** ═══════

Calories	155	Total Fat	3 g	Cholesterol	23 mg
Calories from Fat	15%	Saturated Fat	1 g	Sodium	213 mg

CHOCOLATE CREAM CHEESE CAKE

The ultimate chocolate fantasy. Since this recipe makes three coffeecakes, bake one to eat, one to freeze and one to give away.

non-stick cooking spray
2 packages dry yeast, 1/4-ounces each
1/2 cup very warm water
1 cup nonfat milk
2 tablespoons light margarine
1/2 cup sugar
1 teaspoon salt
1/4 cup cocoa
5 to 5 1/2 cups all-purpose flour, divided
2 eggs

Filling
1 8-ounce package fat-free cream cheese
1/2 cup sugar
1 teaspoon vanilla extract
2 egg whites, beaten

Glaze
1 cup confectioners sugar
2 tablespoons plus 1 teaspoon nonfat milk
1/4 teaspoon vanilla extract
1/4 cup sliced almonds, toasted

In a small bowl, mix yeast with very warm water. Allow to sit for 10 minutes. In a medium-sized saucepan, mix milk with margarine, sugar and salt. On the stove, heat to 135° F, very hot but not boiling. Pour into a large bowl. With electric mixer, beat in cocoa and 1 cup flour until well-blended. Add eggs and yeast mixture, blending well. Add remaining flour and beat with a mixer or knead by hand until dough is smooth and satiny, about five to eight minutes. Spray a large bowl with non-stick cooking spray. Place dough in bowl. Cover and let rise in a warm, draft-free place until doubled, about 1 hour.

To make filling, in a medium-sized mixing bowl, combine cream cheese, sugar, vanilla extract and egg whites. Mix until well-blended. Refrigerate until ready to use.

Preheat oven to 350° F. Spray three 9-inch pie pans with non-stick cooking spray. Roll dough onto a lightly floured surface. Divide into 3 equal portions and let rest for 10 minutes. Roll each portion into a circle, 12 inches in diameter. Place a circle of dough across each prepared pie pan. Dough will hang over edges of pans.

Spread 1/3 of filling onto dough in each pan. At 1-inch intervals, make partial cuts in dough hanging over edge of the pans, leaving dough "flaps" attached. Fold each flap over the next, continuing around in a circle until all flaps overlap on top of filling. Set aside to rise in a warm, draft-free place until doubled, about 40 minutes. Bake 25 minutes or until lightly browned. Cool.

To make glaze, blend confectioners sugar with milk and vanilla extract in a small bowl. When cakes have cooled, drizzle with glaze and sprinkle with almonds.

Makes three cakes. Each cake serves six.

SERVES 18 — **NUTRITIONAL INFORMATION PER SERVING** —

| Calories | 171 | Total Fat | 3 g | Cholesterol | 9 mg |
| Calories from Fat | 20% | Saturated Fat | 1 g | Sodium | 123 mg |

Ices, Sorbets, Gelati & Toppings

Made with fruits, juices or flavorings, the recipes in this chapter are consistently delicious but vary dramatically in texture and taste. From simple and refreshing Ices to smooth and creamy Gelati, frozen delights are great for any occasion.

CHOCOLATE RASPBERRY SORBET

A delicious combination of flavors and textures.

1 cup sugar
2 cups water
2 cups raspberries, fresh or frozen
2 tablespoons cocoa powder

1 egg white, at room temperature
mint sprigs for garnish

In a medium-sized saucepan, blend sugar with water. Heat to boiling. Stir until all of the sugar has dissolved into syrup. Cool. Pour half the mixture into a blender. Add raspberries and purée until almost smooth. Pour into a shallow pan and freeze.

Add cocoa to remaining half of syrup. Heat, stirring to dissolve all cocoa. Remove from heat. In a small bowl, beat egg white until soft peaks form. When chocolate mixture has cooled, fold in egg white until mixture is very smooth. Pour into a shallow pan and freeze.

To serve, remove raspberry sorbet from freezer. Allow to soften. Scoop into a chilled bowl, and beat with electric mixer until smooth. Refreeze for 10 minutes. Scoop into 8 dessert glasses or plates. Remove chocolate sorbet from freezer and scoop beside the raspberry sorbet. Garnish with mint.

SERVES: 8 ═══════ **NUTRITIONAL INFORMATION PER SERVING** ═══════

Calories	110	Total Fat	< 1 g	Cholesterol	0 mg
Calories from Fat	2%	Saturated Fat	< 1 g	Sodium	8 mg

TROPICAL SORBET

Try this recipe with any combination of the delicious tropical fruits available in the markets—mango, papaya, kiwi, pineapple, guava, passionfruit or star fruit.

1/2 cup sugar
1 cup water
1 1/2 cups soft, peeled tropical fruit

1 cup carbonated water
a sprinkle of coconut for garnish

In a medium-sized saucepan, blend sugar with water. Heat to boiling. Stir until all sugar has dissolved into syrup. Cool. In a blender, process fruit with carbonated water until smooth. Pour into syrup, blending until smooth.

Freeze in an ice cream maker following manufacturer's directions. If you do not have an ice cream maker, place in a shallow pan in your freezer. When sorbet has frozen completely, empty into a bowl, beat with an electric mixer until smooth and refreeze until serving. When ready to serve, scoop into 6 serving dishes and garnish with a little coconut.

SERVES: 6 ═══ NUTRITIONAL INFORMATION PER SERVING ═══

Calories	194	Total Fat	0 g	Cholesterol	0 mg
Calories from Fat	0%	Saturated Fat	0 g	Sodium	2 mg

TANGY PEPPERED SORBET

This tasty sorbet is for the adventurous palate.

1 cup sugar
2 cups water
1/3 cup freshly squeezed lime juice
  (2-3 limes)
1/4 cup hot pepper jelly

1 teaspoon lime zest,
  plus additional for garnish
1 1/4 cups carbonated water
lime slices and hot red bird pepper,
  slivered, for garnish

In a medium-sized saucepan, blend sugar with water. Heat to boiling. Stir until all sugar has dissolved into syrup. Cool. Blend in lime juice, jelly, lime zest and water. Mix until smooth.

Freeze mixture in an ice cream maker following manufacturer's directions.

If you do not have an ice cream maker, place mixture in a shallow pan in your freezer. When completely frozen, empty sorbet into a bowl. Beat with an electric mixer until smooth, and refreeze until serving. To serve, scoop into 8 serving dishes. Garnish with lime slices, lime zest and slivered pepper.

SERVES: 6 ━━━━━━ **NUTRITIONAL INFORMATION PER SERVING** ━━━━━━

Calories	160	Total Fat	< 1 g	Cholesterol	0 mg
Calories from Fat	< 1%	Saturated Fat	< 1 g	Sodium	12 mg

CHOCOLATE ICE

🕐 *A delicious chocolate refresher with just one gram of fat.*

1 cup water
1/2 cup sugar
2 tablespoons cocoa

1 tablespoon chocolate morsels
1 cup strong coffee, brewed
16 nonfat chocolate cookies

In a medium-sized pan, heat water and sugar for 10 minutes, stirring occasionally. Mix in cocoa, chocolate morsels and coffee. Pour into eight serving bowls and freeze. Before serving, arrange cookies around each dish.

SERVES: 8		NUTRITIONAL INFORMATION PER SERVING			
Calories	74	Total Fat	1 g	Cholesterol	< 1 mg
Calories from Fat	1%	Saturated Fat	< 1 g	Sodium	3 mg

LEMON ICE

🕐 *This classic hot-weather favorite is a terrific wrap-up to any meal.*

1 cup freshly squeezed lemon juice
  (4-5 lemons)
2 cups water
1/4 teaspoon lemon zest

1/2 cup sugar
thinly sliced lemon peel for garnish
mint leaves for garnish
6 fat-free lemon cookies

In a small mixing bowl, blend lemon juice with water, lemon zest and sugar. Let mixture sit for a few minutes. With an electric mixer or by hand, beat until smooth and all of the sugar has dissolved. Pour into shallow pans and freeze until firm, about 2 hours. Soften ice by removing from freezer five minutes before serving. Scoop fruit ice into 6 dessert glasses. Garnish with lemon peel and mint and serve immediately with cookies.

SERVES: 6		NUTRITIONAL INFORMATION PER SERVING			
Calories	85	Total Fat	0 g	Cholesterol	0 mg
Calories from Fat	0%	Saturated Fat	0 g	Sodium	28 mg

FRUIT ICE

🕐 *Use your favorite fruit juice for this basic ice.*

1 cup fruit juice (cranberry, orange,
   grapefruit, pineapple or guava)
1/3 cup sugar

2 cups water
mint leaves for garnish

In a small mixing bowl, blend juice with sugar and water. Let mixture sit for a few minutes. With an electric mixer or by hand, beat until smooth and all sugar has dissolved. Pour into shallow pans and freeze until firm, about 2 hours.

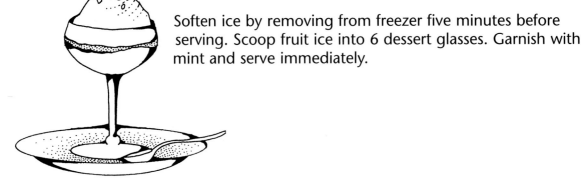

Soften ice by removing from freezer five minutes before serving. Scoop fruit ice into 6 dessert glasses. Garnish with mint and serve immediately.

SERVES: 6 ═══════ **NUTRITIONAL INFORMATION PER SERVING** ═══════

Calories	60	Total Fat	0 g	Cholesterol	0 mg
Calories from Fat	0%	Saturated Fat	0 g	Sodium	1 mg

APPLE SNOW

This classic palate-pleaser is a sweet and delicate refresher.

1 6-ounce can evaporated skim milk
1 tablespoon gelatin
1/3 cup apple juice
1/2 cup sugar, divided

2 teaspoons freshly squeezed
   lemon juice
1 8-ounce jar apple sauce
1 tablespoon slivered almonds,
   toasted, for garnish

Pour evaporated milk into a medium-sized bowl. Place in the freezer along with beaters. Chill until ice crystals form around edges of bowl.

Soak gelatin in apple juice. Place in the top of a double boiler with very hot water in the bottom. Melt softened gelatin over the hot water. Remove from heat. Add 1/4 cup sugar, lemon juice and apple sauce.

Remove beaters and bowl of evaporated milk from freezer. Add remaining sugar and whip milk until mixture is thick and holds peaks. Add gelatin mixture, beating vigorously as the cold will cause the gelatin to harden.

Pour into 6 dessert glasses or bowls. Garnish with almonds. Freeze until ready to serve, at least 1 hour.

SERVES: 6	NUTRITIONAL INFORMATION PER SERVING				
Calories	138	Total Fat	1 g	Cholesterol	1 mg
Calories from Fat	5%	Saturated Fat	< 1 g	Sodium	47 mg

BAKED ALASKA

A double-layer cake filled with ice cream and covered with a luscious meringue shell. Baked Alaska is three dessert favorites in one.

1 White Cake (see page 12)
1 quart nonfat frozen yogurt or fat-free
  ice cream, chocolate
Honey Chocolate Sauce
  (see page 112), optional

Meringue
8 egg whites, at room temperature
1 teaspoon cream of tartar
1/2 teaspoon salt
1 cup sugar
1 teaspoon vanilla extract

Bake two 8-inch rounds as directed in White Cake recipe. Cool. Place one cake round top-side down on an oven-proof platter. Soften ice cream and spread in a circle on one of the layers starting 1 inch in from the edge. Cover and freeze.

To make meringue, in a large, clean bowl, use an electric mixer to whip egg whites with cream of tartar and salt until the mixture is foamy. Sift sugar into egg whites, 1 tablespoon at a time, continuing to whip on high-speed until stiff peaks form. Make sure all sugar has been incorporated into the egg whites. (You can tell this by pinching a bit of the whipped egg white between your fingers. If sugar has been incorporated, you will feel no grains.) Fold in vanilla extract.

Preheat oven to 350° F. Fifteen minutes before serving, remove cake round from freezer and top ice cream layer with the plain cake round. Spread meringue over the entire cake, making sure to seal the seam where the two layers and ice cream meet. Bake until golden brown, about 5 minutes. Slice into 12 wedges and if desired, serve with a dollop of Honey Chocolate Sauce.

SERVES: 12	NUTRITIONAL INFORMATION PER SERVING				
Calories	229	Total Fat	4 g	Cholesterol	0 mg
Calories from Fat	15%	Saturated Fat	< 1 g	Sodium	322 mg

* Nutritional information is based on recipe made without Honey Chocolate Sauce.

CHERRIES JUBILEE

A low-fat version of the famous, flaming restaurant treat.

1 16-ounce can unsweetened cherries
1/4 cup sugar
1/4 cup port wine
1 teaspoon arrowroot

1 teaspoon butter
1 quart nonfat frozen yogurt or
   fat-free ice cream, vanilla
1/4 cup brandy or Cointreau

Drain cherries, reserving juice. In a small saucepan, blend sugar with wine and cherry juice. Simmer until all sugar has been dissolved. Add arrowroot and whisk until sauce has thickened. Add butter, and stir until melted. To serve, scoop ice cream into 4 flame-proof dessert glasses and cover with cherries. Heat brandy slightly in microwave or on stove. Pour onto cherries and carefully ignite.

SERVES: 4		NUTRITIONAL INFORMATION PER SERVING			
Calories	118	Total Fat	1 g	Cholesterol	3 mg
Calories from Fat	8%	Saturated Fat	1 g	Sodium	11 mg

STRAWBERRY CREAM

The perfect topping for strawberry sundae.

1 egg
1/4 cup sugar

1 12-ounce can evaporated skim milk
1/4 cup strawberry preserves

Whisk together egg and sugar in the top of a double boiler with hot water in the bottom. Add evaporated milk and continue to whisk as water boils until the mixture thickens. If the mixture is at all lumpy, pour through a fine strainer and replace in top of double boiler. Add preserves and dissolve. Serve hot or cold with nonfat frozen yogurt, gelati, sorbet or pound cake.

SERVES: 6		NUTRITIONAL INFORMATION PER SERVING			
Calories	133	Total Fat	2 g	Cholesterol	73 mg
Calories from Fat	12%	Saturated Fat	1 g	Sodium	88 mg

GELATI IN A CHOCOLATE PUDDLE

When a sauce is "puddled", it is placed under the dessert, not on top of it, making for an unusual presentation.

3 cups nonfat milk

3/4 cup sugar

1 vanilla bean

Honey Chocolate Sauce (below)

In a medium-sized saucepan over medium-low heat, stir together milk, sugar and vanilla bean. Continue to cook, without boiling, for 5 minutes. Cool. Remove vanilla bean. Pierce one side of bean with a sharp knife and scrape seeds into milk and sugar mixture. Freeze in an ice cream maker following manufacturer's directions. If you do not have an ice cream maker, place mixture in a shallow pan in your freezer. When completely frozen, empty Gelati into a bowl. Beat with an electric mixer, and refreeze until serving. Before serving, puddle Honey Chocolate Sauce on 6 dessert plates. Top with scoops of gelati.

SERVES: 6		NUTRITIONAL INFORMATION PER SERVING			
Calories	173	Total Fat	< 1 g	Cholesterol	4 mg
Calories from Fat	4%	Saturated Fat	< 1 g	Sodium	101 mg

HONEY CHOCOLATE SAUCE

A rich, new twist in a chocolate sauce.

1 6-ounce can evaporated skim milk

1/3 cup honey

1/4 cup corn syrup

3 tablespoons cocoa powder

2 tablespoons creme de cacao

(delicious, but optional)

In a small saucepan, heat milk with honey and corn syrup. Heat until simmering but do not boil. Add cocoa powder, stirring until dissolved. Remove from heat. Add creme de cacao, if desired. Cool. Serve with nonfat frozen yogurt, gelati, sorbet or pound cake.

SERVES: 8		NUTRITIONAL INFORMATION PER SERVING			
Calories	93	Total Fat	< 1 g	Cholesterol	1 mg
Calories from Fat	2%	Saturated Fat	< 1 g	Sodium	33 mg

LIGHT LEMON SAUCE

Try this with the lighter sorbets and gelati desserts.

1 cup water
1/2 cup sugar
1 tablespoon arrowroot
1/2 teaspoon lemon zest

2 tablespoons freshly squeezed
  lemon juice
1 tablespoon butter

In a small saucepan, blend water with sugar and arrowroot. As the mixture heats, whisk until sauce is smooth and thick. Blend in lemon zest and lemon juice. Stir in butter and remove from heat. Serve hot or cold with nonfat frozen yogurt, gelati, sorbet or pound cake.

SERVES: 6		NUTRITIONAL INFORMATION PER SERVING			
Calories	120	Total Fat	1 g	Cholesterol	2 mg
Calories from Fat	7%	Saturated Fat	1 g	Sodium	6 mg

PINEAPPLE SAUCE

Try this sauce on Tropical Sorbet or create contrast by serving it over Chocolate Ice.

1 12-ounce can pineapple
  tidbits, drained
1 tablespoon cornstarch
1/4 teaspoon cinnamon

1/4 cup brown sugar, packed
1 teaspoon freshly squeezed lemon juice
1 tablespoon butter

Drain pineapple, reserving juice (there should be about 1/2 cup). In a heavy, medium-sized saucepan, blend cornstarch with cinnamon and sugar. With a whisk, blend pineapple juice and lemon juice into sugar mixture. When just smooth, add pineapple and stir in butter. Remove from heat. Serve hot or cold with nonfat frozen yogurt, gelati, sorbet or pound cake.

SERVES: 4		NUTRITIONAL INFORMATION PER SERVING			
Calories	116	Total Fat	1 g	Cholesterol	3 mg
Calories from Fat	8%	Saturated Fat	1 g	Sodium	15 mg

SPICY CINNAMON SAUCE

Delicious with apple or coffee-flavored nonfat frozen yogurt or fat-free ice cream.

1 cup apple juice
1/2 cup sugar
1 tablespoon arrowroot
1/2 teaspoon lemon zest

1 teaspoon cinnamon
1/2 teaspoon ground nutmeg
1/2 teaspoon ground cloves
1 tablespoon butter

In a small saucepan, blend apple juice with sugar and arrowroot. As the mixture heats, whisk until sauce is smooth and thick. Blend in lemon zest, cinnamon, nutmeg and cloves. Add butter and continue stirring. Remove from heat. Serve hot or cold with nonfat frozen yogurt, gelati, sorbet or pound cake.

SERVES: 6		NUTRITIONAL INFORMATION PER SERVING			
Calories	120	Total Fat	1 g	Cholesterol	2 mg
Calories from Fat	7%	Saturated Fat	1 g	Sodium	6 mg

BUTTERSCOTCH SAUCE

For a darker and more intensely flavored sauce, use dark corn syrup and the darkest brown sugar available.

1/2 cup brown sugar, packed
1/2 cup corn syrup
1 6-ounce can evaporated skim milk

1 tablespoon butter
1 teaspoon vanilla extract
1/8 teaspoon salt

In a medium-sized sauce pan, blend sugar with corn syrup and milk. Heat to almost boiling, then reduce heat and simmer for 10 minutes. Add butter, vanilla extract and salt. Stir until butter melts. Cool. Serve with nonfat frozen yogurt, gelati, sorbet or pound cake.

SERVES: 6		NUTRITIONAL INFORMATION PER SERVING			
Calories	140	Total Fat	1 g	Cholesterol	5 mg
Calories from Fat	9%	Saturated Fat	1 g	Sodium	90 mg

HOT BANANA RUM SAUCE

A smooth sauce with a tropical flair and a festive flame. If you ignite the rum, the flaming process will burn out any alcohol. If you don't want to use alcohol, rum extract tastes fine but cannot be ignited.

2 ripe bananas
1 tablespoon butter, melted
1 tablespoon dark brown sugar

1 tablespoon freshly squeezed
    lemon juice
1/4 cup dark rum or
    1 tablespoon rum extract

Process bananas with butter, sugar and lemon juice in a blender until very smooth. Pour into a small saucepan and heat, further blending the sugar, banana and butter mixture. Scoop fat-free ice cream or nonfat frozen yogurt into 6 serving bowls. To serve without flame, blend rum or rum extract into the banana mixture and spoon onto ice cream. To serve flaming, pour room-temperature banana sauce over ice cream without adding rum. Heat rum slightly in microwave or on stove. Spoon over sauce and carefully ignite. Make sure to use flame-proof bowls.

SERVES: 6 ══════ **NUTRITIONAL INFORMATION PER SERVING** ══════

Calories	60	Total Fat	1 g	Cholesterol	3 mg
Calories from Fat	2%	Saturated Fat	< 1 g	Sodium	12 mg

Custards, Cremes & Puddings

Ranging from cozy comfort puddings to elegant after-dinner flans, the following recipes are all moist in texture, delicate in flavor and have very little fat.

ALMOND CUSTARD

A smooth and creamy dessert with toasted almond flavoring.

non-stick cooking spray	1/4 cup sugar
2 cups skim milk	1 teaspoon almond extract
1 egg	1/4 teaspoon cinnamon
2 egg whites	2 teaspoons slivered almonds, toasted

Preheat oven to 325° F. Spray four oven-safe, glass custard cups with non-stick cooking spray.

Pour milk into a 1-quart saucepan. Heat until milk is scalded but not boiled. In a large bowl, use an electric mixer or a wire whisk to whip egg and egg whites until frothy. Add sugar and almond extract, beating well. Slowly add the hot milk and whisk until just blended. Pour 3/4 cup of custard into each of the glass custard cups. Place custard cups in a 13 x 9 x 2-inch baking pan. Pour very hot water into the pan around cups so that water and custard levels are even. Carefully place pan with water and custards into oven. Bake 35 minutes or until custard is set. Sprinkle with cinnamon and almonds. Allow custards to rest for 30 minutes before serving.

SERVES: 4 ══════ **NUTRITIONAL INFORMATION PER SERVING** ══════

Calories	127	Total Fat	3 g	Cholesterol	55 mg
Calories from Fat	18%	Saturated Fat	1 g	Sodium	107 mg

CHERRY CUSTARD

The comfort of creamy custard with a fresh fruit taste.

non-stick cooking spray
1 egg
2 egg whites
1 12-ounce can evaporated skim milk
1/2 cup sugar

2 teaspoons vanilla extract
1/8 teaspoon salt
1/2 cup fresh sweet cherries, pitted or
   canned cherries, drained and rinsed

Preheat oven to 350° F. Spray six 6-ounce custard cups with non-stick cooking spray.

In a large bowl, use an electric mixer to combine all ingredients except for cherries. Pour into custard cups. Divide cherries into 6 parts and drop into custard cups. Place custard cups in a 13 x 9 x 2-inch baking pan. Pour boiling water into pan around cups so that water and custard levels are even. Bake 45 to 50 minutes or until a knife inserted into the center of a custard comes out clean. Cool and release custards by placing a plate over each cup and inverting the custard cup onto plate.

SERVES: 6 ===== **NUTRITIONAL INFORMATION PER SERVING** =====

Calories	136	Total Fat	1 g	Cholesterol	38 mg
Calories from Fat	7%	Saturated Fat	< 1 g	Sodium	140 mg

RICE CUSTARD

This lovely recipe is adapted from a very heavy version of Jericalla de Arroz.

non-stick cooking spray
3 eggs, separated
3 cups nonfat milk
1/2 cup plus 1/3 cup sugar, divided
1/2 teaspoon salt

1/4 teaspoon vanilla extract
1 cup cooked white rice
1/2 teaspoon cream of tartar
cinnamon for garnish

Preheat oven to 350° F. Spray a 2-quart baking pan with non-stick cooking spray. In a medium-sized bowl, whisk egg yolks with milk. Stir in 1/2 cup sugar, salt, vanilla extract and rice. Pour into baking pan. Bake 30 minutes or until center is firm. Set aside to cool. In a medium-sized bowl, beat egg whites with cream of tartar until frothy. Sift remaining 1/3 cup sugar, 1 tablespoon at a time, into the egg whites, beating until stiff peaks form. Spread on top of cooled pudding and bake 10 minutes or until meringue is golden brown. To serve, spoon onto dessert plates and sprinkle with cinnamon.

SERVES: 8 ═══ **NUTRITIONAL INFORMATION PER SERVING** ═══

Calories	172	Total Fat	2 g	Cholesterol	81 mg
Calories from Fat	11%	Saturated Fat	1 g	Sodium	72 mg

CREME BRULÉE

An elegant dessert with a delicious crackly crust.

3 12-ounce cans evaporated skim milk
1/3 cup sugar
1/2 teaspoon vanilla extract

2 eggs
2 egg whites
3/4 cup brown sugar

In a very heavy saucepan, blend milk, sugar, vanilla extract, eggs and egg whites. Whisk mixture over a moderate heat until it coats a wooden spoon, about 7 to 10 minutes. Pour into an ungreased, shallow 1 1/2 quart baking pan and stir to cool. Cover with plastic wrap and cool to room temperature, then chill until cold, 1 to 2 hours.

Before serving, heat broiler. Make a bed of crushed ice in a 2-inch deep casserole dish. Remove baking pan from refrigerator and place in bed of ice. Sprinkle top with a 1/4-inch layer of brown sugar. Cook in broiler for 3 minutes, 6 to 8 inches away from the heat source. Make sure sugar caramelizes but does not burn. Remove from ice and allow to set for 15 minutes before serving. Make sure all portions have some of the brown sugar topping on them. Spoon onto dessert plates and serve.

SERVES: 8 ═══ NUTRITIONAL INFORMATION PER SERVING ═══

| Calories | 205 | Total Fat | 1 g | Cholesterol | 57 mg |
| Calories from Fat | 6% | Saturated Fat | 1 g | Sodium | 146 mg |

ZABAGLIONE

🕐 *This Italian custard is soft, flavorful and terrific with fresh fruit.*

3 whole eggs
2/3 cup sugar
pinch salt

2/3 cup Marsala wine (dealcoholized wine may be substituted)
1 teaspoon slivered almonds, toasted, for garnish

Crack eggs into the top of an unheated double boiler. Whip with a wire whisk. Sprinkle sugar, a little at a time, into eggs, beating well after each addition. Beat in salt and wine. Heat water in the bottom of the double boiler to a simmer. Set top of the double boiler over, not in, the simmering water. Continue beating until custard is thick and foamy, about 5-7 minutes. The Zabaglione may be served warm or cool. If served cool, whisk it occasionally so that it does not separate. Serve in six 6-ounce wine glasses. Garnish with toasted almonds or dollops of fruit purée.

Variation
CHOCOLATE ZABAGLIONE: Blend 2 tablespoons cocoa powder with sugar. Sift this mixture into the eggs as directed above and proceed with traditional Zabaglione recipe but eliminate almonds. Serves: 6
Calories 121; calories from fat 19%; total fat 3 g; saturated fat 1 g; cholesterol 107 mg; sodium 33 mg

SERVES: 6		NUTRITIONAL INFORMATION PER SERVING			
Calories	121	Total Fat	3 g	Cholesterol	107 mg
Calories from Fat	20%	Saturated Fat	1 g	Sodium	33 mg

MEXICAN BREAD PUDDING

Apple and cheese give this bread pudding its kick.

1 small, day-old loaf French bread
  (about 8 ounces)
1 tablespoon chopped walnuts, toasted
1/2 cup raisins
1 tart apple
  (such as Granny Smith), chopped

1/3 cup cheddar cheese
1 cup brown sugar, packed
1 1/2 cups water
1 teaspoon cinnamon
1 teaspoon orange zest
orange slices for garnish

Tear the bread into 1/2 inch cubes. Allow to dry overnight or toast in oven at 200° F for 1 hour.

Preheat oven to 350° F. In a 2-quart baking pan, Layer half the bread with half the walnuts, raisins, apple and cheese. Repeat. In a medium-sized saucepan, blend sugar, water, cinnamon and orange zest. Bring to a boil for 5 minutes. Pour over bread cubes and bake 40 to 45 minutes or until bread has absorbed all syrup. To serve, spoon onto dessert plates and garnish with orange slices.

SERVES: 10 ═══ **NUTRITIONAL INFORMATION PER SERVING** ═══

Calories	194	Total Fat	3 g	Cholesterol	4 mg
Calories from Fat	12%	Saturated Fat	1 g	Sodium	157 mg

ESPRESSO WHIP

This recipe is easy and ultra-light.

1 15-ounce container nonfat
  ricotta cheese
1/2 cup confectioners sugar
2 tablespoons dark rum or
  1 teaspoon rum extract

2 tablespoons espresso or
  strong coffee, cold
1 tablespoon sweetened cocoa powder

In a medium-sized bowl, combine ricotta cheese with sugar, rum and espresso. Whip with an electric mixer until all ingredients are smooth. Spoon mixture into four 6-inch dessert glasses. Chill until firm, about 2 hours. To serve, dust with sweetened cocoa.

SERVES: 4		NUTRITIONAL INFORMATION PER SERVING			
Calories	114	Total Fat	< 1 g	Cholesterol	1 mg
Calories from Fat	1%	Saturated Fat	< 1 g	Sodium	68 mg

CRANBERRY WHIP

Keep a couple of bags of cranberries in your freezer and make this delicious recipe any time.

2 cups fresh or frozen cranberries
2 cups water, divided
1/2 cup apple juice

1 cup sugar
1/3 cup farina or quick-cooking tapioca
mint sprigs for garnish

In a medium-sized sauce pan, blend cranberries with 1 cup water and apple juice. Simmer until cranberries cook and pop. Cool slightly before pressing through a strainer or a food mill to remove skins. Pour cranberry juice back into pan. Add sugar and remaining water. Heat to boiling and add farina or tapioca, whisking constantly until thickened, 1 to 2 minutes. Cool slightly and beat with an electric mixer until whip becomes fluffy and pink. Pour into 6 dessert glasses or a serving bowl. Cool completely and garnish with mint sprigs.

SERVES: 6		NUTRITIONAL INFORMATION PER SERVING			
Calories	145	Total Fat	1 g	Cholesterol	0 mg
Calories from Fat	4%	Saturated Fat	< 1 g	Sodium	1 mg

RICE PUDDING

🕐 *Smooth and rich tasting, this recipe is also very low in fat.*

1 cup brown rice, cooked according to
  package directions
1 cup evaporated skim milk
1/2 cup plus 2 tablespoons sugar,
  divided

1 teaspoon cinnamon
1/4 teaspoon allspice
1/4 teaspoon nutmeg
1 cup raisins
4 egg whites

Preheat oven to 300° F. In a large bowl, combine rice with milk, 1/2 cup sugar, cinnamon, allspice, nutmeg and raisins.

In a separate bowl, use an electric mixer or a whisk to beat egg whites until frothy. Add remaining sugar, a tablespoon at a time, and continue beating egg whites until soft peaks form. Gently fold into rice mixture. Pour into an ungreased 9-inch square baking pan. Bake 20 to 30 minutes or until rice is set. Serve with fresh fruit or fruit sauce.

SERVES: 8   **NUTRITIONAL INFORMATION PER SERVING**

Calories	230	Total Fat	1 g	Cholesterol	1 mg
Calories from Fat	3%	Saturated Fat	< 1 g	Sodium	68 mg

TAPIOCA PUDDING

A starch from the cassava root, tapioca is a delicious way to thicken desserts. This recipe and the following variations utilize "fish eye" or pearl tapioca.

1/3 cup large pearl tapioca
1 cup water
2 cups nonfat milk

1/3 cup sugar
1/4 teaspoon salt
1/4 teaspoon vanilla extract

In a large saucepan, soak tapioca in cup of water for several hours or overnight. After soaking, add milk, sugar and salt. Stir and heat to a simmer. Simmer (do not boil) for 1 hour, stirring occasionally. Remove from heat and fold in vanilla extract. Pour into 4 dessert glasses and cool completely before serving.

SERVES: 4	NUTRITIONAL INFORMATION PER SERVING					
Calories	127	Total Fat	1 g	Cholesterol	1 mg
Calories from Fat	1%	Saturated Fat	< 1 g	Sodium	81 mg

BAKED TAPIOCA

Try this recipe for a more richly flavored tapioca.

1/3 cup large pearl tapioca
1 cup water
non-stick cooking spray
2 cups nonfat milk

1/3 cup sugar
1 teaspoon salt
1/4 teaspoon vanilla extract
2 teaspoons butter

In a large saucepan, soak tapioca in cup of water for several hours or overnight. Preheat oven to 325° F. Spray a non-stick 1-quart baking pan with non-stick cooking spray. After soaking, add milk, sugar and salt. Stir and heat to a simmer. Simmer (do not boil) for 30 minutes, stirring occasionally. Pour tapioca into prepared baking pan. Stir in vanilla extract and butter. Bake 1 hour or until the top is nicely browned. Cool before serving.

SERVES: 4	NUTRITIONAL INFORMATION PER SERVING					
Calories	108	Total Fat	2 g	Cholesterol	7 g
Calories from Fat	18%	Saturated Fat	1 g	Sodium	216 mg

BUTTERSCOTCH TAPIOCA

A rich flavor twist to old comfort food.

1/3 cup large pearl tapioca
1 cup water
2 cups nonfat milk
1/3 cup sugar

1 teaspoon salt
2 tablespoons butter
3/4 cup brown sugar,
    granulated not brownulated

In a large saucepan, soak tapioca in cup of water for several hours or overnight. After soaking, add milk, sugar and salt. Stir and heat to a simmer. In a medium-sized saucepan, heat butter and sugar. Stir until mixture melts. Pour into tapioca. Simmer (do not boil) for 1 hour, stirring occasionally. Pour into 6 dessert glasses and cool completely before serving.

SERVES: 6 ======= **NUTRITIONAL INFORMATION PER SERVING** =======

Calories	196	Total Fat	4 g	Cholesterol	12 mg
Calories from Fat	18%	Saturated Fat	2 g	Sodium	178 mg

QUICK COOKING TAPIOCA

🕐 *Just twenty-five minutes start to finish*

1/2 cup sugar
3 tablespoons quick-cooking tapioca
2 3/4 cups nonfat milk

1 egg, beaten
1 teaspoon vanilla extract

In a medium-sized saucepan, whisk sugar, tapioca, milk and egg. Heat to a full boil, stirring constantly. Remove from heat and whisk in vanilla extract. Cool for 20 minutes stirring several times. Spoon into six 6-ounce dessert dishes or into a serving bowl. Serve warm or cold.

Variations

QUICK BUTTERSCOTCH TAPIOCA: Melt brown sugar in butter as in recipe for Butterscotch Tapioca. Blend into boiled tapioca mixture. Omit vanilla extract. Serves: 6
Calories 205; calories from fat 16%; total fat 4 g; saturated fat 2 g; cholesterol 36 mg; sodium 87 mg

CHOCOLATE TAPIOCA: Sift 2 tablespoons cocoa powder into pan with sugar, tapioca, milk and egg. Omit vanilla extract. Serves: 6
Calories 141; calories from fat 8%; total fat 1 g; saturated fat < 1 g; cholesterol 37 mg; sodium 70 mg

SERVES: 6		NUTRITIONAL INFORMATION PER SERVING			
Calories	137	Total Fat	1 g	Cholesterol	37 mg
Calories from Fat	7%	Saturated Fat	< 1 g	Sodium	68 mg

BASIC BLANCMANGE

A blancmange is a thick, cornstarch based pudding that's low-fat and delicious. In preparing this recipe, it is crucial to use a heavy bottomed saucepan which conducts heat well, to cook over a very low heat so that the pudding doesn't scorch, and to use a whisk that fits the saucepan well.

4 cups nonfat milk
6 tablespoons cornstarch
2/3 cup sugar

2 teaspoons vanilla extract
2 cups berries (fresh strawberries,
    blueberries, or raspberries)

In a heavy saucepan, over a low heat, whisk together the milk and cornstarch. Add sugar gradually and continue to whisk until mixture thickens, about 5 to 7 minutes. Fold in vanilla extract. Pour into a 1 1/2-quart mold which has been rinsed with cold water. Chill until firm. To serve, release blancmange from large mold onto a serving platter and garnish with fruit. Spoon onto dessert plates.

Variations
CHOCOLATE BLANCMANGE: Blend cornstarch with 3 tablespoons cocoa powder. Proceed as above. Serves: 8
Calories 130; calories from fat 2%; total fat < 1 g; saturated fat < 1 g; cholesterol 2 mg; sodium 65 mg

FRUIT BLANCMANGE: Use 2 cups puréed fruit and decrease milk to 2 cups. Proceed as above. Serves: 8
Calories 116; calories from fat 2%; total fat < 1 g; saturated fat < 1 g; cholesterol 1 mg; sodium 33 mg

SERVES: 8		NUTRITIONAL INFORMATION PER SERVING			
Calories	137	Total Fat	< 1 g	Cholesterol	2 mg
Calories from Fat	2%	Saturated Fat	< 1 g	Sodium	64 mg

VANILLA PUDDING

🕐 *This soft and creamy pudding is very easy to adapt.*

2 tablespoons cornstarch	1 egg, beaten
1/2 cup sugar	1 teaspoon vanilla extract
2 cups nonfat milk	1 teaspoon butter or margarine

In a heavy saucepan, whisk together cornstarch and sugar. Gradually add milk and continue to whisk. Heat, stirring constantly, until mixture just boils. Turn heat to low and blend a little of the hot mixture into the egg to heat it. Pour heated egg into pudding and whisk vigorously. Cook for 2 to 3 more minutes or until pudding is thick and creamy. Fold in vanilla extract and butter. Pour into serving dishes and serve warm or cover well with plastic, chill and serve cold.

Variations
PUMPKIN PUDDING: Whisk in 1/2 cup pumpkin purée with sugar. Increase eggs to 2. Continue as directed. Serves: 8
Calories 136; calories from fat 15%; total fat 3 g; saturated fat 1 g; cholesterol 74 mg; sodium 70 mg

FRUIT PUDDING: Whisk in 1/2 cup fruit purée with sugar. Increase eggs to 2. Continue as directed. Serves: 8
Calories 137; calories from fat 16%; total fat 3 g; saturated fat 1 g; cholesterol 74 mg; sodium 70 mg

CHOCOLATE PUDDING: Sift 2 tablespoons cocoa with sugar. Continue as directed. Serves: 8
Calories 120; calories from fat 13%; total fat 2 g; saturated fat 1 g; cholesterol 39 mg; sodium 60 mg

SERVES: 6 ═══════ **NUTRITIONAL INFORMATION PER SERVING*** ══════

Calories	117	Total Fat	2 g	Cholesterol	39 mg
Calories from Fat	12%	Saturated Fat	1 g	Sodium	59 mg

* Nutritional information based on recipe made with butter.

PINEAPPLE FLAN

The caramel goodness of flan with a refreshing tropical flavor.

non-stick cooking spray
1/2 cup sugar

Flan
1 3-ounce can pineapple tidbits
1/2 cup water (approximately)
1 egg

2 egg whites
1 12-ounce can evaporated skim milk
1/3 cup sugar
1/4 teaspoon vanilla extract
1/4 teaspoon almond extract
1/8 teaspoon salt

Preheat oven to 350° F. Spray six 6-ounce custard cups with non-stick cooking spray. In a small non-stick frying pan, melt sugar until it is browned and caramelized. Spoon into 6 prepared custard cups. As syrup hardens, rotate cups to coat sides with caramel.

To make flan, drain pineapple, reserving syrup in measuring cup. Add water to pineapple syrup to make 3/4 cup. In a large mixing bowl, use an electric mixer to combine pineapple with egg, egg whites, milk, pineapple, syrup, sugar, vanilla extract, almond extract and salt. Pour mixture into custard cups, dividing evenly. Place cups in a 13 x 9 x 2-inch baking pan. Pour boiling water into pan around custard cups so that water and custard levels are even. Bake 45 to 50 minutes or until a knife inserted into center of flan comes out clean. Cool and release flan by placing a plate over each cup and inverting flan onto plate.

SERVES: 6 ══════ **NUTRITIONAL INFORMATION PER SERVING** ══════

Calories	149	Total Fat	1 g	Cholesterol	37 mg
Calories from Fat	5%	Saturated Fat	< 1 g	Sodium	108 mg

Mousses, Meringues & Soufflés

Capturing the wonderful flavors of fresh fruit, the recipes in this chapter are very light; with low calorie counts and very little fat. Experiment, using fruits in season and replacing strawberries with equal amounts of blueberries, oranges with bananas or cocoa powder with flavored extracts. Use your imagination and enjoy.

COFFEE MOCHA MOUSSE

Smooth, delicious and melts in your mouth.

1 6-ounce can evaporated skim milk
1/4 cup hot coffee, freshly brewed
1/4 cup cocoa powder

2 eggs, separated, at room temperature
4 tablespoons sugar, divided

Pour evaporated milk into a medium-sized bowl. Put in freezer along with beaters. Chill until ice crystals begin forming around edges of bowl.

In another medium-sized bowl, combine coffee with cocoa. Beat in egg yolks. In a small, very clean bowl, beat egg whites until frothy. Gradually add 2 tablespoons sugar, 1 tablespoon at time, beating until soft peaks form.

Remove bowl from freezer and whip evaporated milk with remaining sugar until mixture is thick and holds peaks. Fold in egg white and coffee mixtures. Spoon into six 1/2-cup dessert glasses. Freeze until ready to serve.

SERVES: 6 ══════ **NUTRITIONAL INFORMATION PER SERVING** ══════

Calories	95	Total Fat	2 g	Cholesterol	72 mg
Calories from Fat	19%	Saturated Fat	< 1 g	Sodium	56 mg

FROZEN CHOCOLATE MOUSSE

An elegant and frosty chocolate delight.

1 6-ounce can evaporated skim milk	1/8 teaspoon salt
1 tablespoon gelatin	1 cup nonfat milk
1/3 cup cold water	3/4 cup sugar, divided
1/4 cup cocoa powder	1/4 cup slivered almonds, toasted

Pour evaporated milk into a medium-sized bowl. Put in freezer along with beaters. Chill until ice crystals begin forming around edges of bowl.

Soak gelatin in cold water until soft. Place in the top of a double boiler with very hot water in the bottom. Melt softened gelatin over the hot water. Remove from heat. Add cocoa, salt, nonfat milk and 1/2 cup plus 2 tablespoons sugar.

Remove bowl from freezer. Whip evaporated milk with remaining sugar until mixture is thick and holds peaks. Add gelatin mixture and beat vigorously as the cold will cause gelatin to harden. Fold in almonds, reserving a few for garnish. Pour into 6 sherbet glasses and freeze for at least 2 hours.

SERVES: 6 ═══ **NUTRITIONAL INFORMATION PER SERVING** ═══

Calories	155	Total Fat	3 g	Cholesterol	1 mg
Calories from Fat	16%	Saturated Fat	< 1 g	Sodium	10 mg

BERRY SOUFFLÉ

Any berry or combination of berries will do, frozen or fresh.

non-stick cooking spray
4 tablespoons sugar, divided
2 tablespoons cornstarch
1/8 teaspoon salt
1 cup berry purée (raspberry,
 strawberry, or blueberry)

1 1/2 teaspoons vanilla extract
1 teaspoon orange liqueur
 or orange extract
6 egg whites, at room temperature
1/2 teaspoon cream of tartar

Preheat oven to 425° F. Spray an 8-inch soufflé or oven-proof dish with non-stick cooking spray and sprinkle with 1 tablespoon sugar. In a medium-sized saucepan, combine cornstarch, salt, berry purée, vanilla extract, orange flavoring and remaining sugar. Over medium heat, whisk until this sauce thickens. Pour into a large mixing bowl.

In a large, clean bowl, beat egg whites until frothy. Add cream of tartar and beat until stiff peaks form. Blend a third of the egg white mixture into berry sauce in large mixing bowl. Then, fold berry sauce into the egg white mixture. This should take about 20 strokes. Pour into prepared dish and smooth surface with spatula.

As soon as the soufflé has been placed in the oven, reduce heat to 375° F and bake 20 minutes or until top is browned and soufflé is firm to the touch.

SERVES: 6 **NUTRITIONAL INFORMATION PER SERVING**

Calories	57	Total Fat	< 1 g	Cholesterol	0 mg
Calories from Fat	2%	Saturated Fat	< 1 g	Sodium	58 mg

CITRUS SOUFFLÉ

Mandarin oranges make this a delicate delight.

non-stick cooking spray
1 15-ounce can mandarin oranges
1/4 cup sugar
1 teaspoon vanilla extract
zest of 1 lemon

2 tablespoons orange liqueur
  or orange extract
8 egg whites
1 teaspoon cream of tartar

Preheat oven to 425° F. Spray a 2-quart soufflé dish with non-stick cooking spray.

Drain syrup from mandarin oranges into a measuring cup. If you don't have a full cup of syrup, make up the difference with water. In a small saucepan, combine this liquid with sugar, vanilla extract, lemon zest and orange flavoring. Heat to dissolve sugar. Pour into blender, add mandarin oranges and purée. In a large clean bowl, beat egg whites until frothy. Add cream of tartar and continue beating until stiff peaks form. Blend a third of the egg whites into the orange purée. Then, fold purée into the egg white mixture. This should take about 20 strokes. Pour into prepared dish and smooth surface with a spatula.

As soon as the dish has been placed in the oven, reduce heat to 375° F. Bake 20 minutes, or until the top is browned and soufflé is firm to the touch.

SERVES: 8 ═══ **NUTRITIONAL INFORMATION PER SERVING** ═══

| Calories | 48 | Total Fat | < 1 g | Cholesterol | 0 mg |
| Calories from Fat | 1% | Saturated Fat | < 1 g | Sodium | < 1 mg |

LEMON SOUFFLÉ

A tangy and delightful finish to any meal.

non-stick cooking spray
1/3 cup light margarine
1/4 cup nonfat milk
2/3 cup sugar, divided
1 teaspoon lemon zest

2 tablespoons freshly squeezed
   lemon juice
1 egg
6 egg whites
orange and lemon slices for garnish

Preheat oven to 400 ° F. Spray a 2-quart soufflé dish with non-stick cooking spray.

Melt margarine in a medium-sized saucepan. With a whisk, beat in milk and 1/3 cup sugar. Cook until thickened and smooth. Remove from heat and stir in lemon zest and lemon juice. In a small bowl, use an electric mixer to beat whole egg with 2 egg whites until thick and well-blended. Add to thickened sauce.

In a large, clean bowl, beat remaining egg whites until frothy. Sprinkle remaining sugar, 1 tablespoon at a time, into egg whites, beating until stiff peaks form. Add sauce to egg whites, folding gently to blend. Pour into prepared dish and bake 55 to 60 minutes or until top is browned and soufflé is firm to the touch. Garnish with lemon and orange slices.

SERVES: 8	NUTRITIONAL INFORMATION PER SERVING		
Calories	150	Total Fat	2 g	Cholesterol	27 mg
Calories from Fat	14%	Saturated Fat	< 1 g	Sodium	86 mg

PRALINE SOUFFLÉ

Sweet and flavorful, this dessert may be prepared 2 hours ahead of time. Bake just before serving.

Praline
1/2 cup sugar
2 tablespoons pecans,
  very finely chopped

Soufflé
non-stick cooking spray
8 egg whites
1 whole egg

1 1/2 cups nonfat milk
1/3 cup cornstarch
1 teaspoon vanilla extract
1 1/4 cups sugar, divided
1 tablespoon dark rum or
  1/2 teaspoon rum extract
1 teaspoon cream of tartar

To prepare praline, In a small saucepan over high heat, melt and stir sugar until it turns a deep caramel color. Add pecans and stir until they are well-coated. Carefully pour the mixture onto a piece of aluminum foil to cool. Finely crush cooled praline with a hammer or with a food processor.

Preheat oven to 400 ° F. Spray a large soufflé dish with non-stick cooking spray. To make Soufflé, in a heavy saucepan, whisk 2 egg whites, the whole egg, milk, cornstarch, vanilla extract and 1 cup sugar. Stir constantly and add rum. Cook over moderate heat to make a smooth, very thick custard. Remove from heat.

In a separate bowl, beat the remaining egg whites with cream of tartar until frothy. Continue beating until stiff peaks form, gradually adding the remaining 1/4 cup of sugar, 1 tablespoon at a time. Stir 1/3 of the egg white mixture into the custard to lighten it; then fold egg white mixture into custard.

Pour into prepared soufflé dish. Top with praline. Bake 30 to 35 minutes or until soufflé has risen and is lightly browned on top.

SERVES: 8 ═══ **NUTRITIONAL INFORMATION PER SERVING** ═══

Calories	303	Total Fat	2 g	Cholesterol	37 mg
Calories from Fat	6%	Saturated Fat	< 1 g	Sodium	117 mg

PUMPKIN SOUFFLÉ

A great dessert for Thanksgiving or anytime.

non-stick cooking spray
10 egg whites, at room temperature
1/2 teaspoon cream of tartar
1/2 cup sugar, sifted
1 cup cake flour, sifted

1/2 cup pumpkin purée
1/3 cup water
1 teaspoon cinnamon
1/2 teaspoon nutmeg
1/4 teaspoon cloves

Preheat oven to 350° F. Spray a 10-inch tube pan with non-stick cooking spray. Place egg whites in a warm, clean, large bowl. With an electric mixer, beat at high speed until frothy. Add cream of tartar and continue beating, adding sugar, 1 tablespoon at a time, until egg whites are stiff and satiny. In a separate bowl, blend flour, with pumpkin purée, water and spices. Carefully fold into egg white mixture, about 20 or 30 strokes. Pour into tube pan. Bake 50 to 55 minutes or until cake is firm to the touch. Remove from oven and invert pan, cooling the soufflé upside down in the pan. When the soufflé is completely cooled, run a knife around the edges to loosen it from pan. Remove inverted soufflé onto serving dish and serve.

SERVES: 12 ===== **NUTRITIONAL INFORMATION PER SERVING** =====

Calories	108	Total Fat	< 1 g	Cholesterol	0 mg
Calories from Fat	2%	Saturated Fat	< 1 g	Sodium	93 mg

CHOCOLATE MERINGUE

Shape this meringue into a bowl for frozen yogurt or ice cream.

12 x 16-inch piece of brown paper
  (a paper bag works well)
2/3 cup sugar
1/3 cup cocoa powder
6 egg whites, at room temperature

1/2 teaspoon cream of tartar
8 scoops nonfat frozen yogurt or fat-
  free ice cream
berries and mint sprigs for garnish

Preheat oven to 200° F. Place brown paper on a baking sheet. Sift sugar and cocoa powder together. Set aside. In a separate bowl, whip egg whites with an electric mixer. Blend in cream of tartar. When egg whites are frothy, sprinkle sugar-cocoa mixture, a tablespoon at a time, into egg whites. Continue to beat egg whites until stiff, incorporating sugar well. (You can tell this by pinching a bit of the whipped egg white between your fingers. If sugar has been incorporated, you will feel no grains.) Empty mixture onto brown paper. Form meringue into a bowl-shape, hollowing-out center and making sure to maintain about even thickness. Bake for 12 hours.

To serve, put ice cream scoops into meringue shell. Freeze until ready to serve. Garnish with berries and mint leaves.

SERVES: 8	NUTRITIONAL INFORMATION PER SERVING				
Calories	133	Total Fat	< 1 g	Cholesterol	0 mg
Calories from Fat	3%	Saturated Fat	0 g	Sodium	42 mg

STRAWBERRY MERINGUES

Turn fresh strawberries into an after-dinner delight.

12 x 16-inch piece of brown paper
  (a paper bag works well)
6 egg whites, at room temperature
1/2 teaspoon cream of tartar

2/3 cup sugar
1 quart strawberries,
  stemmed and sliced
8 mint sprigs for garnish

Preheat oven to 200° F. Place brown paper on a baking sheet. Whip egg whites with an electric mixer. Blend in cream of tartar. When egg whites are frothy, sprinkle 1/3 cup sugar, a tablespoon at a time, into egg whites. Continue beating egg whites until stiff, incorporating sugar well. (You can tell this by pinching a bit of the whipped egg white between your fingers. If sugar has been incorporated, you will feel no grains.) In batches, put mixture into a pastry bag. Squeeze 8 beehive-shaped meringues onto brown paper. Bake for 12 hours. Remove and store in a sealed plastic bag until serving.

To serve, mix strawberries with remaining sugar. Put 1/2 cup strawberries into small bowl and top with meringue, or put all strawberries into a large oval serving bowl and top with all 8 meringues.
Garnish with mint sprigs.

SERVES: 8	NUTRITIONAL INFORMATION PER SERVING				
Calories	95	Total Fat	< 1 g	Cholesterol	0 mg
Calories from Fat	< 1%	Saturated Fat	0 g	Sodium	42 mg

Cuban Natillas— page 179

Espresso Whip— page 124

Honey Chocolate Sauce—page 112

Lemon Ice & Fruit Ice— pages 107 & 108

Top: Zabaglione—page 122
Left to right: Apple Carrot Muffins—page 92   Coffee Mocha Mousse—page 134

French Baked Fruit Dessert— page 166

Gingerbread— page 185

Chocolate Pops— page 192

Sweets From Around The World

Desserts are often the most important part of
celebrations and many family traditions. Here's a
collection of favorite recipes from around the
world adapted to today's light eating style.

Serve Middle Eastern Honey Cake on festive occasions. Pool raspberry purée onto dessert plates, top with a slice of cake and garnish with nonfat whipped topping and a slivered almond or two.

MIDDLE EASTERN HONEY CAKE

Honey and spices contribute to a cake that's bursting with flavor.

non-stick cooking spray
1 1/2 cups all-purpose flour
3/4 cup sugar
1 teaspoon baking powder
1 teaspoon cinnamon
1/2 teaspoon salt
1/4 teaspoon ground nutmeg
3/4 cup milk

2 tablespoons vegetable oil
1 egg

Syrup
1/4 cup sugar
1/4 cup water
1/4 cup honey
1 teaspoon lemon juice

Preheat oven to 350° F. Spray a 9-inch round cake pan with non-stick cooking spray. In a large bowl, blend flour with sugar, baking powder, cinnamon, salt and nutmeg. Beat in milk, oil and egg. Beat on medium for 2 minutes, scraping bowl and blending well. Pour into prepared pan. Bake 35 to 40 minutes or until a toothpick inserted in the center comes out clean. Cool.

To make syrup, in a small pan, heat sugar with water, honey and lemon juice. Simmer for 5 minutes. Pour syrup onto cooled cake. Cut into six slices and serve.

SERVES: 6 ════ **NUTRITIONAL INFORMATION PER SERVING** ════

Calories	173	Total Fat	3 g	Cholesterol	18 mg
Calories from Fat	15%	Saturated Fat	< 1 g	Sodium	133 mg

GREEK FRUIT AND NUT BAKLAVA

A splendid variation of the classic Greek dessert.

non-stick cooking spray
9 filo sheets, defrosted and
  wrapped in a damp dish towel
2 tablespoons butter, melted

Apple & Nut Mixtures
2 apples, quartered, cored and chopped
4 tablespoons sugar, divided
1 tablespoon freshly squeezed
  lemon juice

1 teaspoon cinnamon, divided
2 tablespoons walnuts, coarsely ground

Syrup
2/3 cup sugar
1 tablespoon honey
1/2 cup water
1 strip lemon peel
1 cinnamon stick

To make syrup, combine 2/3 cup sugar, honey, water, lemon peel and cinnamon stick in medium-sized saucepan. Bring to a boil, lower heat and simmer until slightly thickened, about 15 minutes. Remove from heat and let cool.

To make apple and nut mixtures, in a medium-sized mixing bowl, combine apples, 3 tablespoons sugar, lemon juice and 3/4 teaspoon cinnamon. Gently mix together. In a small bowl, blend nuts with remaining sugar and cinnamon.

Spray a 13 x 9 x 3-inch baking pan with non-stick cooking spray. Lay one sheet of filo in prepared pan, brush lightly with butter and fold sheet in half to fit pan. Add 2 more sheets, brushing each with butter and folding over from alternating sides to fit pan. Spread half of apple mixture evenly over the filo. Follow by laying out 2 more sheets of filo, folding each to fit the pan and brushing with butter between layers. Sprinkle nuts over this layer. Cover with another sheet of filo, brushing with butter and doubling it over. Spread remaining apples over this layer. Follow with the three remaining sheets of filo, folding each sheet to fit pan and brushing with butter between layers. Cut off excess filo dough to give baklava an even-edge. Brush top with remaining butter.

Refrigerate unbaked baklava for about 30 minutes. This makes it easy to score the pieces prior to baking. Preheat oven to 350° F. Using a sharp knife, cut 20 diamond shaped pieces. Bake 25 minutes, reduce heat to 300° F and bake an additional 15 to 20 minutes or until golden brown. While warm, pour cooled syrup over baklava. Cool before serving.

1 PER SERVING		NUTRITIONAL INFORMATION PER SERVING			
Calories	80	Total Fat	2 g	Cholesterol	7 mg
Calories from Fat	18%	Saturated Fat	1 g	Sodium	12 mg

CANADIAN BLUEBERRY SUPREME

🕐 *A popular Canadian dessert brimming with fresh blueberries.*

4 cups fresh blueberries
2 tablespoons apple juice
1 tablespoon cornstarch
2/3 cup sugar, divided

2/3 cup oat bran cereal or
  oatmeal, uncooked
1/2 cup all-purpose flour
1 tablespoon margarine, softened
1/4 cup corn syrup

Preheat oven to 350° F. In a medium-sized bowl, mix blueberries with apple juice, cornstarch and 1/3 cup sugar. Spread into bottom of 2-quart baking pan. Blend remaining sugar with oat bran, flour, margarine and corn syrup. Spread over blueberries. Bake until filling is bubbly and topping is brown and crusty, about 40 minutes.

SERVES: 6		NUTRITIONAL INFORMATION PER SERVING			
Calories	183	Total Fat	1 g	Cholesterol	0 mg
Calories from Fat	7%	Saturated Fat	< 1 g	Sodium	22 mg

AFRICAN AKWADU

🕐 *Bananas, a staple in Africa, are the main ingredient in this delicious fruit dessert.*

non-stick cooking spray
1/3 cup lime juice
1/2 cup apple juice
1 teaspoon coconut extract
1/4 cup brown sugar, packed

5 bananas, peeled and split lengthwise
1 tablespoon butter
1 teaspoon unsweetened
   shredded coconut

Preheat oven to 375° F. Spray a 9-inch baking pan with non-stick cooking spray. Combine lime juice, apple juice, coconut extract and sugar in a medium-sized bowl and stir until sugar dissolves.

Arrange bananas in baking pan. Pour sauce over the bananas and dot with butter. Bake eight to ten minutes or until bananas are just heated through. Garnish lightly with shredded coconut.

SERVES: 6		NUTRITIONAL INFORMATION PER SERVING			
Calories	142	Total Fat	3 g	Cholesterol	6 mg
Calories from Fat	18%	Saturated Fat	2 g	Sodium	66 mg

GERMAN PLUM DUMPLINGS

Serve low-fat yet scrumptious dumplings for an unexpected treat.

non-stick cooking spray
1 cup potato, baked, peeled and
   mashed (1 large potato)
1 egg
1 tablespoon butter, melted
1/2 teaspoon salt

3/4 cup all-purpose flour
3 fresh plums or 6 canned plum halves
6 sugar cubes
1 egg white, lightly beaten
1/4 cup sugar
1/4 teaspoon cinnamon

Preheat oven to 350° F. Spray a 9-inch baking pan with non-stick cooking spray. In a medium-sized mixing bowl, combine potato with egg, butter, salt and flour and blend well. Shape into a disc and allow to rest on a cutting board for 5 minutes. Roll dough into an 8 x 12-inch rectangle. Cut into six 4-inch squares.

Cut fresh plums in half and remove pit. Leave skins on plums. Put 1 sugar cube into the center of each plum half. Place a plum half in the center of each square of dough. Bring corners together and moisten with egg white to seal. Carefully place dumplings into baking pan. Brush the tops and sides of dumplings with remaining egg white and sprinkle generously with cinnamon and sugar. Bake 30 to 35 minutes or until pastry is browned.

SERVES: 6		NUTRITIONAL INFORMATION PER SERVING			
Calories	184	Total Fat	3 g	Cholesterol	41 mg
Calories from Fat	18%	Saturated Fat	2 g	Sodium	209 mg

JEWISH KUGEL

🕐 *A sweet and creamy noodle pudding. Tastes terrific chilled.*

non-stick cooking spray
1 cup nonfat sour cream
1 cup nonfat cottage cheese
1 cup white raisins, plumped by
   steaming over boiling water
   for 5 minutes
1/2 cup sugar

1/2 teaspoon cinnamon
1/4 teaspoon nutmeg
1 teaspoon salt
1 cup nonfat milk
1 8-ounce package wide noodles,
   cooked and drained

Preheat oven to 350° F. Spray a 2-quart casserole dish with non-stick cooking spray. In a large bowl, blend all ingredients except noodles. Gently stir in noodles and turn mixture into prepared pan. Bake 45 to 50 minutes or until golden brown. Serve hot, at room temperature or chilled.

SERVES: 8		NUTRITIONAL INFORMATION PER SERVING			
Calories	181	Total Fat	< 1 g	Cholesterol	< 1 mg
Calories from Fat	5%	Saturated Fat	< 1 g	Sodium	237 mg

CARIBBEAN BANANA BAKE

🕐 *Traditionally, this recipe is made with the guanabana, unavailable in most American markets. Bananas make a fine replacement in this savory dessert.*

non-stick cooking spray
6 tablespoons fat-free cream cheese,
   softened
1/4 cup brown sugar, packed
1/4 cup dark rum or
   1 tablespoon rum extract

3 tablespoons evaporated skim milk
1/2 teaspoon cinnamon
5 medium-ripe bananas
1 tablespoon butter

Preheat oven to 325° F. Spray a 1-quart casserole dish with non-stick cooking spray. Combine cream cheese, brown sugar, rum, milk and cinnamon in a blender and process until very smooth. Slice half the bananas into casserole dish. Dot with butter and top with half of the cream cheese mixture. Cover with a second layer of banana slices and top with remaining cream cheese mixture. Bake 25 minutes or until sauce is hot and bubbly and cheesecake filling is firm.

SERVES: 6	NUTRITIONAL INFORMATION PER SERVING					
Calories	64	Total Fat	1 g	Cholesterol	3 mg
Calories from Fat	13%	Saturated Fat	1 g	Sodium	38 mg

MIDDLE EASTERN SEMOLINA PUDDING

Semolina, commonly used for pasta, adds texture and flavor to this pudding. Semolina is available in Mediterranean markets and some large grocery stores.

1 1/2 cups water
1/2 cup sugar
2 tablespoons butter
1/4 cup corn syrup
3/4 cup semolina

1/2 cup raisins
1 tablespoon slivered almonds, toasted
1/8 teaspoon salt
freshly grated nutmeg

In a small pan, heat water with sugar and corn syrup. Boil until sugar is dissolved into syrup, about 10 minutes. In a large saucepan, blend butter with semolina. Cook over low heat until semolina browns, about 5 minutes. Blend syrup into semolina mixture . Add raisins, almonds and salt. Cook for 10 minutes, stirring constantly, until mixture becomes very thick. Spoon into six 6-ounce dessert dishes. Sprinkle with nutmeg and serve.

SERVES: 6		NUTRITIONAL INFORMATION PER SERVING			
Calories	159	Total Fat	2 g	Cholesterol	4 mg
Calories from Fat	12%	Saturated Fat	1 g	Sodium	90 mg

DANISH RICE PUDDING WITH RASPBERRIES

Make this creamy and satisfying dessert in advance, allowing it plenty of time to chill.

1 6-ounce can evaporated skim milk
2 tablespoons gelatin
1/2 cup cold water
1/2 cup sugar, divided

1 1/2 cups cooked rice
1 teaspoon vanilla extract
1 1/2 cups raspberries
1/4 cup currant jelly

Pour evaporated milk into a medium-sized bowl and place in freezer along with beaters. Chill until ice crystals form around edges of bowl.

Soak gelatin in cold water until soft. Place in top of double boiler with very hot water in bottom. Melt softened gelatin over hot water. Remove from heat and stir in 1/4 cup sugar. Chill until mixture is syrupy.

Remove bowl of evaporated milk from freezer and whip milk with vanilla and remaining sugar. When mixture is thick and will hold peaks, add gelatin mixture. Beat vigorously as the cold mixture will cause the gelatin to harden. Fold in cooked rice. Scoop into a 1 1/2-quart tube or bundt pan. Cover and refrigerate until firm, about 3 hours. Loosen and release pudding from mold onto serving plate.

Put raspberries and currant jelly into blender and process until smooth. Spoon sauce onto 8 small dessert plates and top with portions of rice pudding.

SERVES: 8		NUTRITIONAL INFORMATION PER SERVING			
Calories	144	Total Fat	< 1 g	Cholesterol	< 1 mg
Calories from Fat	2%	Saturated Fat	< 1 g	Sodium	32 mg

AUSTRALIAN MERINGUE PAVLOVA

A lightened-up version of the traditional Pavlova, named for Russian ballerina Anna Pavlova.

brown paper bag or parchment paper
4 egg whites, at room temperature
1/2 teaspoon cream of tartar
1/4 teaspoon salt
3/4 cup sugar
1/2 teaspoon vanilla extract
1 6-ounce can evaporated skim milk

Frosting
1 tablespoon gelatin
1/3 cup cold water
2 tablespoons sugar
1 cup sliced kiwi or other fruit
Juice of 1 lemon

Preheat oven to 225° F. Cut paper to fit bottom of a round, 9-inch cake pan.

In a large, clean mixing bowl, whip egg whites with cream of tartar and salt until mixture is foamy. Sift 3/4 cup sugar, 2 tablespoons at a time, into egg whites, continuing to whip on high speed until stiff peaks form. Make sure all sugar has been incorporated into the egg whites. (You can tell by pinching a bit of whipped egg white between your fingers. If sugar has been incorporated, you will feel no grains.) Fold in vanilla extract.

Pour meringue into prepared pan. Cut gently through batter with a knife to remove any large bubbles. Bake for 1 1/2 hours, then turn off oven, leaving meringue in oven with door closed for at least 1 hour. With a knife, loosen edge of meringue from pan, then tap pan to release. Invert onto a serving plate.

Pour evaporated milk into a medium-sized bowl and place in freezer along with beaters. Chill until ice crystals form around edges of bowl. To make frosting, soak gelatin in cold water until soft. Place in the top of a double boiler with very hot water in bottom. Melt softened gelatin over hot water. Remove from heat and add remaining sugar. Chill in the freezer until mixture is syrupy.

Remove bowl from freezer and whip evaporated milk until it is thick and will hold peaks. Add gelatin mixture, beating vigorously as the cold mixture will cause the gelatin to harden. Frost top and sides of meringue cake with gelatin frosting. Freeze cake until 1/2 hour before serving time.

Immediately before serving, squeeze lemon juice onto sliced fruits so that they do not brown. Decorate frosted cake with fruit and serve.

SERVES: 8		NUTRITIONAL INFORMATION PER SERVING			
Calories	119	Total Fat	0 g	Cholesterol	0 mg
Calories from Fat	0%	Saturated Fat	0 g	Sodium	31 mg

CHINESE COOKIES: TEEM GOK

These sweet, crunchy cookies are baked, not fried.

1 1/4 cups dried fruit, chopped
  (any combination of apricots, raisins,
  apples, banana chips or figs)
3/4 cup brown sugar, packed
1/2 cup nonfat granola

1 tablespoon shredded coconut
1 tablespoon chopped almonds
48 small wonton wraps (available in
  most produce departments)
1 tablespoon butter, melted

Preheat oven to 400° F. Steam dried fruit until soft and moist, about five minutes, in a steamer over boiling water. Remove fruit from heat and chop finely. In a medium bowl, mix with brown sugar, granola, coconut and almonds.

Place an undersized tablespoon of filling on each egg wrap. Wrap in ends and fold over. Place onto ungreased cookie sheet. Repeat with remaining egg wraps. Recipe makes 48 cookies. Brush with melted butter and bake until golden brown, about five to seven minutes. Cool and serve or store in an air-tight container.

1 PER SERVING		NUTRITIONAL INFORMATION PER SERVING			
Calories	29	Total Fat	< 1 g	Cholesterol	2 mg
Calories from Fat	12%	Saturated Fat	< 1 g	Sodium	9 mg

ENGLISH PLUM PUDDING WITH HARD SAUCE

A thoroughly English holiday tradition. Make sure that the water doesn't boil away as it's essential to keep this steamed pudding moist.

non-stick cooking spray
1/2 cup all-purpose flour
1 teaspoon allspice
1 cup raisins
1/2 cup currants
1/2 cup chopped candied fruits
2 tablespoons chopped walnuts, toasted
3/4 cup soft bread crumbs
1 tablespoon vegetable oil

1/2 cup brown sugar, packed
2 eggs
6 cups boiling water

Hard Sauce
1 teaspoon butter, softened
1 cup confectioners sugar
2 tablespoons nonfat milk
1/4 cup brandy

Preheat oven to 225° F. Spray a 4-cup fluted mold with non-stick cooking spray. In a large mixing bowl, combine flour with allspice, raisins, currants, candied fruits, walnuts and bread crumbs. In a separate bowl, blend vegetable oil with sugar and eggs. Mix wet ingredients into dry ingredients until just blended. Pour into prepared pan.

Place pan in a Dutch oven. Pour boiling water into Dutch oven around pudding pan and cover with piece of aluminum foil. Put into oven. Bake, keeping water boiling, for 3 hours or until a toothpick inserted into center of pudding comes out clean. Cool. Loosen sides from pan and invert onto a flame-proof serving plate.

Make hard sauce by blending butter with confectioners sugar and milk.

To serve, heat brandy just slightly in microwave or on stove. Pour over pudding and ignite. Serve hard sauce atop pudding or on the side.

SERVES: 8 ═══════ **NUTRITIONAL INFORMATION PER SERVING** ═══════

Calories	219	Total Fat	3 g	Cholesterol	36 mg
Calories from Fat	16%	Saturated Fat	1 g	Sodium	72 mg

FRENCH BABA AU RHUM

Soaked in savarin syrup this delectable cake will stay moist for days.

non-stick cooking spray
1 package dry yeast, 1/4-ounce
1/2 cup very warm water
2 tablespoons vegetable oil
1/3 cup corn syrup
4 eggs, beaten
1/2 teaspoon salt
2 cups all-purpose flour, divided

1/2 cup golden raisins

Savarin Syrup
1/2 cup sugar
1/2 cup water
2 tablespoons rum or
   1 teaspoon rum extract

Preheat oven to 375° F. Spray a 10-inch tube pan with non-stick cooking spray.

In a large bowl, blend yeast with warm water. Set aside for 5 minutes or until bubbly. Stir in oil, corn syrup, eggs, salt, 1 cup flour and raisins. Beat, adding remaining flour to make a very smooth batter. Pour into prepared pan. Cover and set in a warm place to rise for 30 minutes. This will lighten the batter and allow it to bake more evenly. Bake 30 minutes or until golden brown. Cool cake 10 minutes before removing it from pan onto a serving platter.

Make Savarin Syrup in a small saucepan by blending sugar, water and rum. Simmer over heat until sugar is dissolved. Remove from heat to cool. Drizzle syrup over cake, allowing all of it to be absorbed. Garnish with fresh fruit and serve.

SERVES: 12 ══════════ **NUTRITIONAL INFORMATION PER SERVING** ══════

Calories	195	Total Fat	4 g	Cholesterol	53 mg
Calories from Fat	17%	Saturated Fat	1 g	Sodium	114 mg

FRENCH BAKED FRUIT DESSERT

🕐 *Fresh fruit makes this simple dish a French country delicacy.*

non-stick cooking spray
2 cups fresh fruit (strawberries,
  blueberries, raspberries,
  sweet cherries or a combination)
3 eggs

1 cup nonfat milk
1/3 cup sugar
1/2 cup all-purpose flour
1 teaspoon almond extract

Preheat oven to 350° F. Spray an 8-inch round cake pan with non-stick cooking spray. Spread fruit over the bottom of prepared baking pan. In a medium-sized mixing bowl, combine eggs, milk, sugar, flour and almond extract and blend until very smooth. Pour over fruit. Bake 45 minutes or until crust is golden brown. Serve immediately.

SERVES: 6 ═══ **NUTRITIONAL INFORMATION PER SERVING** ═══

Calories	188	Total Fat	3 g	Cholesterol	164 mg
Calories from Fat	18%	Saturated Fat	1 g	Sodium	32 mg

REVANI (GREEK YOGURT CAKE)

Yogurt keeps this scrumptious Greek cake light without adding fat.

non-stick cooking spray
2 tablespoons unsalted butter
1 egg, separated
1/2 cup sugar
1 teaspoon brandy or vanilla extract
1/2 cup nonfat yogurt
1 1/4 cups cake flour, sifted twice
1/2 teaspoon baking soda
2 egg whites

Syrup
1/2 cup sugar
1 tablespoon honey
1/3 cup water
1 strip lemon peel
1 cinnamon stick

Preheat oven to 350° F. Spray an 8-inch round cake pan with non-stick cooking spray.

Use an electric mixer to cream butter with egg yolk, sugar and brandy. Add yogurt and mix well. Sift together flour and baking soda in a small bowl. Mix dry ingredients, a little at a time, into wet ingredients until fully blended. In a separate bowl, beat egg whites with electric mixer until stiff peaks form. Fold into batter. Pour batter into prepared pan. Bake 30 minutes. Cake is done when top is golden brown and springs back when touched.

To make syrup, combine sugar with honey, water, lemon and cinnamon in a medium-sized saucepan. Bring to a boil, then lower heat and simmer until slightly thickened, about 15 minutes. Remove from heat to cool.

When it is done baking, pour cooled syrup over it. Cool completely in pan. Cut into 8 wedges and serve.

SERVES: 8 ═══════ **NUTRITIONAL INFORMATION PER SERVING** ═══════

Calories	193	Total Fat	4 g	Cholesterol	34 mg
Calories from Fat	17%	Saturated Fat	2 g	Sodium	109 mg

ENGLISH TRIFLE

Lightened just a bit, this is nearly an authentic version of the distinctive English Trifle. For an even lighter trifle recipe, see page 34.

1/2 cup plus 2 tablespoons sugar,
   divided
3 tablespoons cornstarch
1/8 teaspoon salt
3 cups nonfat milk
1/2 cup sherry (if sherry is not used,
   replace with water)
1 egg
2 egg whites
1 tablespoon butter

1 tablespoon vanilla extract
36 ladyfingers (a light sponge cake
   available at most grocery stores.)
1/2 cup strawberry preserves
1 1/2 cups fresh or frozen strawberries
   or blueberries
1 6-ounce can evaporated skim milk
1 tablespoon gelatin
1/3 cup cold water
1 tablespoon slivered almonds, toasted

Pour evaporated milk into a medium-sized bowl and place in freezer along with beaters. Chill until ice crystals form around edges of bowl.

To make pudding, in a medium-sized saucepan, whisk together 1/2 cup sugar with cornstarch, salt, milk and sherry. Heat to boiling, whisking constantly. Boil for 1 minute before cooling slightly. In a small bowl, beat egg with egg whites. Whisk a little of the hot milk mixture into eggs, then add eggs to saucepan. Return to boil and cook until pudding coats a spoon, about 3 minutes. Remove from heat and stir in butter and vanilla extract. Cool.

Split ladyfingers lengthwise and spread each half with strawberry preserves. In a 2-quart round serving bowl or trifle dish, arrange a layer of ladyfingers, preserves facing up. Spread half of the pudding then half of the strawberries over ladyfingers. Next, stand a ring of ladyfingers upright around the inside wall of the dish, jelly side facing center. Layer additional ladyfingers, remaining pudding, and remaining strawberries into trifle dish. Cover and chill.

Soak gelatin in cold water until soft. Place in top of double boiler with very hot water in bottom. Melt softened gelatin over hot water. Remove from heat. Add remaining sugar. Chill until mixture is syrupy.

Remove bowl of evaporated milk from freezer and whip until mixture is thick and will hold peaks. Add gelatin mixture, beat vigorously as the cold mixture will cause gelatin to harden. Spread on top of trifle, garnish with toasted almonds and refrigerate until serving.

SERVES: 16	NUTRITIONAL INFORMATION PER SERVING				
Calories	251	Total Fat	3 g	Cholesterol	57 mg
Calories from Fat	10%	Saturated Fat	1 g	Sodium	446 mg

GREEK DIPLES

A taste of honey in a crisp little package.

non-stick cooking spray	1/2 teaspoon salt
1 egg	2 1/4 to 2 1/2 cups all-purpose flour
4 egg whites	1/4 cup honey
1 tablespoon vegetable oil	1 teaspoon water
1 teaspoon baking powder	1/8 teaspoon nutmeg

Preheat oven to 400° F. Spray a cookie sheet with non-stick cooking spray. In a medium-sized mixing bowl, mix egg, egg whites, oil, baking powder and salt. Blend in enough flour to make a stiff dough. Knead into a ball and allow to rest for 5 minutes.

On a well-floured surface, roll dough as thin as possible with a rolling-pin. Cut into 32 long, narrow strips about 8 x 1 inch.

Twist or knot the strips and place on prepared cookie sheet. Mix honey with water, and brush on each diple. Sprinkle with nutmeg and bake 5 to 7 minutes or until golden brown.

1 PER SERVING	NUTRITIONAL INFORMATION PER SERVING				
Calories	116	Total Fat	1 g	Cholesterol	< 1 mg
Calories from Fat	4%	Saturated Fat	< 1 g	Sodium	32 mg

INDONESIAN MERINGUE PUDDING

Deliciously seasoned bread pudding with a soft meringue top.

non-stick cooking spray
6 slices wheat bread, cubed
1 16-ounce can crushed pineapple
2 eggs, separated
1 6-ounce can evaporated skim milk
1/3 cup brown sugar, packed

1 teaspoon cinnamon
1 teaspoon coconut extract
2 egg whites
1 teaspoon cream of tartar
1/4 cup sugar

Preheat oven to 350° F. Spray an 8 x 8 x 2-inch square baking pan with non-stick cooking spray. Spread bread cubes over pan bottom. Drain pineapple, reserving juice. Spread pineapple over bread. In a medium-sized mixing bowl, blend pineapple juice with egg yolks, milk, brown sugar, cinnamon and coconut extract. Pour over bread and pineapple already in pan. Bake 30 to 40 minutes or until a toothpick inserted into the middle of the pudding comes out clean. Cool in pan.

In a medium-sized bowl, beat egg whites with cream of tartar until frothy. Sift sugar, 1 tablespoon at a time, into egg whites, beating until peaks just begin forming and all sugar has been incorporated. (You can tell by pinching a bit of whipped egg white between your fingers. If sugar has been incorporated, you will feel no grains.)

Spread meringue over pudding and bake 10 minutes or until meringue is golden brown. Allow to stand a few minutes before cutting.

SERVES: 8 ═══ **NUTRITIONAL INFORMATION PER SERVING** ═══

Calories	190	Total Fat	4 g	Cholesterol	59 mg
Calories from Fat	17%	Saturated Fat	2 g	Sodium	167 mg

MOCHA TORTE

Purchase an angel food cake and turnout this tasty dessert on your busiest day.

1 9-inch angel food cake	2 egg whites, at room temperature
2 tablespoons butter	1 6-ounce can evaporated skim milk
1 1/2 cups confectioners sugar	1 tablespoon gelatin
4 teaspoons nonfat milk	1/3 cup water
4 tablespoons cocoa	2 tablespoons sugar
6 tablespoons strong coffee, cooled	1 teaspoon vanilla extract

Using a serrated knife, cut cake horizontally into 6 layers.

In a large bowl, mix butter, confectioners sugar, milk, cocoa and coffee. In a medium-sized, clean mixing bowl, whip egg whites until light and fluffy. Fold into chocolate-coffee mixture. Spread 1/5 of mixture on bottom layer of angel food cake. Cover with next layer of cake and spread with more mixture. Repeat until all of the mixture and all of cake has been used. Refrigerate.

Pour evaporated milk into a medium-sized bowl and place in freezer along with beaters. Chill until ice crystals form around edges of bowl. Soak gelatin in cold water until soft. Place in top of double boiler with very hot water in bottom. Melt softened gelatin over hot water. Remove from heat. Chill until mixture is syrupy.

Remove bowl of evaporated milk from freezer and whip milk with sugar and vanilla extract. When mixture is thick and will hold peaks, beat in gelatin mixture. Beat vigorously as the cold mixture will cause gelatin to harden. Spread on top and sides of cake. Freeze, allowing 15 to 20 minutes to thaw before serving.

SERVES: 12	NUTRITIONAL INFORMATION PER SERVING				
Calories	184	Total Fat	2 g	Cholesterol	7 mg
Calories from Fat	12%	Saturated Fat	1 g	Sodium	142 mg

DOBOS TORTE

Next to Strudel, this is Hungary's favorite dessert. If four baking pans are not available, bake two cakes at a time, keeping the remaining batter refrigerated.

non-stick cooking spray
3 eggs, separated
1 1/2 cups sugar
1 1/2 cups all-purpose flour
1 teaspoon baking power
1 teaspoon salt
1 cup water
2 teaspoons vanilla extract

6 egg whites
1 teaspoon cream of tartar

Frosting
5 cups confectioners sugar
3 tablespoons cocoa
1 tablespoon butter
3/4 cup nonfat milk

Preheat oven to 325° F. Spray four 8-inch round cake pans with non-stick cooking spray. In a large bowl, beat egg yolks until thick and smooth, about 5 minutes. Beat in sugar, flour, baking powder, salt, water and vanilla extract until well-blended.

In a large bowl, beat egg whites with cream of tartar. Beat until egg whites hold peaks. Fold egg whites into egg yolk mixture. Divide among 4 prepared pans and bake 25 to 35 minutes or until toothpick comes out clean when inserted into the center of each cake. Cool for 5 minutes in pan before turning on to wire racks to cool completely.

In a medium-sized bowl, mix confectioners sugar with cocoa, butter and enough milk to make a thick frosting. Cut each cake horizontally, making a total of 8 layers. Spread frosting between each layer of cake and then frost top and sides of cake. Cut into 16 pieces and serve.

SERVES: 16 ═══ **NUTRITIONAL INFORMATION PER SERVING** ═══

Calories	283	Total Fat	3 g	Cholesterol	32 mg
Calories from Fat	9%	Saturated Fat	1 g	Sodium	207 mg

INDIAN SPICE PUDDING

The bold flavor of cardamom enhances this pudding-like dessert. During preparation, it's very important that the milk never boil.

2 12-ounce cans evaporated skim milk
6 carrots, peeled and shredded
1/2 cup brown sugar, packed
1 teaspoon ground cardamom

1/2 cup raisins
1/4 teaspoons salt
1 tablespoon butter
1 tablespoon chopped pistachio nuts

In a medium-sized saucepan, mix milk with carrots. Heat almost to a boil, then reduce heat to the lowest setting. Cover, stirring frequently, and simmer until all liquid has been absorbed, about 45 minutes to an hour. Stir in sugar, cardamom, raisins, salt and butter. Cook over low heat until sugar is dissolved and pudding is thick. Place in serving bowls, garnish with pistachios and serve immediately.

SERVES: 6 ══════ **NUTRITIONAL INFORMATION PER SERVING** ══════

Calories	153	Total Fat	2 g	Cholesterol	6 mg
Calories from Fat	7%	Saturated Fat	1 g	Sodium	154 mg

TIRAMISU

One of Italy's gifts to the world- a beautiful dessert that melts in your mouth.

1 6-ounce can evaporated skim milk
1 tablespoon gelatin
1/3 cup cold water
3/4 cup plus 1 tablespoon sugar,
   divided
3 egg whites
1/2 teaspoon cream of tartar

1 8-ounce package fat-free cream cheese
1/4 cup espresso or strong
   coffee, cooled
2 tablespoons coffee liqueur
24 ladyfingers (a light sponge cake
   available at most grocery stores.)
1 teaspoon cocoa powder

Place evaporated milk in a medium-sized bowl in freezer along with beaters. Chill until ice crystals form around edges of bowl. Soak gelatin in cold water until soft. Place in top of double boiler with very hot water in bottom. Melt softened gelatin over hot water. Remove from heat. Add 1/4 cup sugar and chill until mixture is syrupy.

Remove bowl of evaporated milk from freezer and whip with electric mixer. When mixture is thick and will hold peaks, add gelatin mixture, beating vigorously as the cold mixture will cause gelatin to harden. Refrigerate.

Clean double boiler and beaters. Combine egg white with cream of tartar in top of double boiler with boiling water in the bottom. Beat with electric mixer until eggs are frothy. Sift remaining sugar, 1 tablespoon at a time, into egg whites, beating until soft peaks form. As mixture heats, peaks will become stiff. Remove from heat. In a medium-sized bowl, beat cream cheese with espresso and coffee liqueur until creamy and well-blended. Fold in the egg whites.

Split lady fingers and arrange half in the bottom of a 9-inch square baking pan. Top with half the gelatin mixture, then half the espresso mixture. Repeat until all ingredients are used. Sprinkle with cocoa. Refrigerate for several hours for flavors to blend. To serve, spoon into dessert dishes.

SERVES: 8 ══════════ **NUTRITIONAL INFORMATION PER SERVING** ══════

Calories	191	Total Fat	3 g	Cholesterol	12 mg
Calories from Fat	14%	Saturated Fat	< 1 g	Sodium	116 mg

JAPANESE AMBROSIA

🕐 *The litchi, with its unique, refreshing flavor, makes this recipe special. Litchis may be found in Asian groceries or in some large supermarkets.*

1 11-ounce can litchis
2 teaspoons freshly squeezed lime juice
1 12-ounce can mandarin
   orange segments

1 tablespoon shredded coconut
thinly sliced lime peel for garnish.

Mix all ingredients together in a medium-sized bowl. Refrigerate until serving time. To serve, divide among six 4-ounce dessert dishes. Garnish with lime peel.

SERVES: 6		NUTRITIONAL INFORMATION PER SERVING			
Calories	119	Total Fat	< 1 g	Cholesterol	< 1 mg
Calories from Fat	3%	Saturated Fat	< 1 g	Sodium	7 mg

DANISH MIXED BERRY PUDDING

🕐 *Cornstarch gives this pudding a sparkling appearance.*

2 cups fresh strawberries, washed
   and hulled
2 cups fresh raspberries, washed
1/2 cup cornstarch
1/4 cup sugar

1 cup cold water
1 tablespoon freshly squeezed lime juice
1 tablespoon chopped, toasted nuts
   for garnish

Purée strawberries in blender and empty into a medium-sized bowl. Purée raspberries in blender and stir into strawberry purée. Set aside. In a medium-sized saucepan, whisk cornstarch with sugar and water. Heat to boiling, stirring constantly. When mixture has thickened, about two or three minutes, reduce heat. Stir in lime juice. Cool slightly and mix in purée. Refrigerate. To serve, divide among six 8-ounce dessert dishes. Garnish with toasted nuts.

SERVES: 6		NUTRITIONAL INFORMATION PER SERVING			
Calories	93	Total Fat	1 g	Cholesterol	0 mg
Calories from Fat	10%	Saturated Fat	< 1 g	Sodium	1 mg

STRAWBERRIES ROMANOF

🕐 *A low-fat version of a luscious dessert once served to Russian royalty.*

1 6-ounce can evaporated skim milk
1 tablespoon gelatin
1/3 cup water
1/4 cup sugar

4 tablespoons kirsch
1 quart strawberries, hulled (reserve a
   few pretty ones for garnish)

Place evaporated milk in a medium-sized bowl in the freezer along with beaters. Chill until ice crystals form around edges of bowl.

Soak gelatin in cold water until soft. Place in top of double boiler with very hot water in bottom. Melt softened gelatin over hot water. Remove from heat. Add 2 tablespoons sugar. Chill until mixture is syrupy.

Remove bowl from freezer and whip with remaining sugar until mixture is thick and will hold peaks. Add gelatin mixture, beating vigorously as the cold mixture will cause gelatin to harden. In a large mixing bowl, mix kirsch and strawberries.

When ready to serve, blend gelatin topping and strawberries. Spoon onto dessert plates or bowls. Garnish with reserved berries.

SERVES: 6	NUTRITIONAL INFORMATION PER SERVING				
Calories	121	Total Fat	< 1 g	Cholesterol	1 mg
Calories from Fat	3%	Saturated Fat	< 1 g	Sodium	38 mg

MEXICAN FLAN

In Italy and France, this dessert is called Creme Caramel. In Spain and Mexico, it's Flan. Coated with caramel sauce, it's always a delicious treat.

non-stick cooking spray
1 egg
2 egg whites
1 12-ounce can evaporated skim milk
1/3 cup sugar

2 teaspoons vanilla extract
1/8 teaspoon salt

Caramel Sauce
1/2 cup sugar

Preheat oven to 350° F. Spray four 6-ounce custard cups with non-stick cooking spray.

In a small non-stick frying pan, heat 1/2 cup sugar until melted. Watch carefully as sugar browns and caramelizes, making sure to not let it burn. Pour into prepared custard cups. Rotate cups to coat with caramel as it hardens.

Mix remaining ingredients in a large bowl with electric beater. Divide among custard cups and place cups in a square baking pan. Pour enough boiling water into pan around custard cups so that the custard and water levels are equal.

Bake 45 to 50 minutes. When cooked, a knife inserted into the center of flan will come out clean. Cool. Release flan from cups by placing a plate over the custard cup and then inverting the custard onto plate. Serve.

SERVES: 4 ═══════ **NUTRITIONAL INFORMATION PER SERVING** ═══════

Calories	187	Total Fat	1 g	Cholesterol	57 mg
Calories from Fat	7%	Saturated Fat	< 1 g	Sodium	408 mg

SWISS MERINGUES

A delicious combination of fresh fruit and fluffy meringues with nearly no fat.

brown paper bag or parchment paper
3 egg whites, at room temperature
1/4 teaspoon cream of tartar
1/2 cup sugar, divided
1 6-ounce can evaporated skim milk

1 tablespoon gelatin
1/3 cup cold water
2 tablespoons confectioners sugar
1 teaspoon vanilla extract
1/1 2 cups berries of your choice

Preheat oven to 225° F. Prepare a baking pan by covering it with brown paper or parchment paper. In a medium-sized bowl, beat egg whites with cream of tartar until frothy. Sift 1/4 cup sugar, 1 tablespoon at a time, into egg whites, beating until peaks just begin to form and all the sugar has been incorporated. (You can tell by pinching a bit of whipped egg white between your fingers. If sugar has been incorporated, you will feel no grains.)

Drop meringue by 1/4 cupfuls onto brown paper. Shape into 8 ovals. Bake for 1 hour and then turn off oven. Leave meringues in oven with the door closed for 1 hour, allowing them to dry completely.

Place evaporated milk in a medium-sized bowl in freezer along with beaters. Chill until ice crystals form around edges of bowl. Soak gelatin in cold water until soft. Place in the top of double boiler with very hot water in bottom. Melt softened gelatin over hot water. Remove from heat. Add confectioners sugar and vanilla extract. Chill until mixture is syrupy.

Remove bowl of evaporated milk from freezer and whip milk with remaining sugar. When mixture is thick and will hold peaks, beat in gelatin mixture. Beat vigorously as the cold mixture will cause gelatin to harden. Refrigerate until serving time. To serve, place meringues on 8 large dessert plates. Divide berries and topping among plates. Serve immediately.

SERVES: 8 ══════ **NUTRITIONAL INFORMATION PER SERVING** ══════

Calories	45	Total Fat	< 1 g	Cholesterol	1 mg
Calories from Fat	15%	Saturated Fat	< 1 g	Sodium	47 mg

CUBAN NATILLAS

A beautiful luscious dessert with the look of a floating cloud.

3 eggs
8 egg whites, divided
1/4 cup all-purpose flour
4 cups nonfat milk, divided

1/2 cup sugar
1/2 teaspoon vanilla extract
berries and mint leaves for garnish

In a medium-sized bowl, beat whole eggs with 4 egg whites. Add flour and blend into a thick paste. Mix in 1 cup of milk and beat until smooth. In a stockpot, blend sugar, vanilla extract and remaining milk. Heat until mixture just begins to boil. Remove from heat and gradually whisk in egg-flour mixture. Return to a low heat and continue to whisk until the mixture thickens, about 5 to 7 minutes. Pour into oven-safe serving dish. Chill.

Pour remaining egg whites into a very clean bowl and beat until frothy. Continue beating until stiff peaks form. Top pudding with meringue and brown under broiler for 5 minutes.

SERVES: 12 ═══════ **NUTRITIONAL INFORMATION PER SERVING** ═══════

Calories	82	Total Fat	< 1 g	Cholesterol	7 mg
Calories from Fat	3%	Saturated Fat	< 1 g	Sodium	80 mg

Just For Kids

Playful in presentation and terrific in taste, kids not only love eating the following desserts, they love helping to make them, too.

BANANA BOYS

Make sure to use ripe bananas. Let the children decorate their cookies with any extra raisins.

non-stick cooking spray
2 tablespoons light margarine
1/2 cup brown sugar, packed
1/3 cup corn syrup
3 egg whites
1/2 teaspoon vanilla extract
3 medium bananas, mashed

2 cups all-purpose flour
1 1/2 teaspoons baking powder
1/2 teaspoon cinnamon
1/2 teaspoon baking soda
1/4 teaspoon salt
1 cup raisins

Preheat oven to 375° F. Spray a cookie sheet with non-stick cooking spray. In a small mixing bowl, cream margarine with brown sugar and corn syrup. Beat in egg whites, vanilla extract and mashed bananas. In a medium-sized bowl, combine flour, baking powder, cinnamon, baking soda and salt. Blend wet ingredients into dry ingredients. Gently fold in 3/4 cup raisins. Drop batter onto prepared sheet by teaspoonfuls about 2 inches apart. With clean, wet hands, smooth batter into rounds. Make faces on the "banana boys" with remaining raisins. Bake 10 to 12 minutes or until cookies are lightly browned.

Makes 50 cookies.

1 PER SERVING		NUTRITIONAL INFORMATION PER SERVING			
Calories	50	Total Fat	< 1 g	Cholesterol	0 mg
Calories from Fat	5%	Saturated Fat	< 1 g	Sodium	32 mg

OATMEAL RAISIN COOKIES

Moist, hearty and delicious.

non-stick cooking spray
1 cup all-purpose flour
3 cups rolled oats
2 teaspoons baking soda
2 teaspoons cinnamon
1/2 cup sugar

1 cup applesauce
1 teaspoon vanilla extract
1 cup raisins, plumped by steaming
   over boiling water for 5 minutes
3 egg whites, whipped with a fork

Preheat oven to 350° F. Spray 2 cookie sheets with non-stick cooking spray.

In a large bowl, combine flour, rolled oats, baking soda, cinnamon and sugar. In a smaller bowl, mix applesauce, vanilla extract, raisins and egg whites. Stir wet ingredients into dry ingredients and mix until thoroughly blended. Drop by large spoonfuls onto prepared cookie sheets. Flatten to about 1/2-inch thick. Bake 10 to 12 minutes or until cookies are lightly browned.

Makes 30 cookies.

1 PER SERVING ═══ **NUTRITIONAL INFORMATION PER SERVING** ═══

Calories	89	Total Fat	1 g	Cholesterol	0 mg
Calories from Fat	6%	Saturated Fat	0 g	Sodium	62 mg

NO BAKE COOKIES II

🕐 *Make delicious and nutritious cookies without even turning on the oven.*

3/4 cup finely-chopped dried fruit
  (raisins, apricots, or dates in any
  combination)
3/4 cup graham cracker crumbs
3/4 cup cereal (corn flakes, crisp rice,
  oat flakes), crushed

1/2 cup confectioners sugar
1/4 cup corn syrup
1 tablespoon orange juice
1/4 cup wheat germ, toasted

Combine fruit, graham cracker crumbs, cereal, sugar, corn syrup and orange juice. With clean hands, shape mixture into 36 balls. Roll balls in wheat germ. These cookies can be stored in a covered container at room temperature. For another No Bake Cookie recipe, see page 85.

Calories	53	Total Fat	1 g	Cholesterol	0 mg
Calories from Fat	13%	Saturated Fat	0 g	Sodium	33 mg

GINGERBREAD

🕐 *Nothing smells quite as good as gingerbread baking. Try serving warm gingerbread with a little nonfat frozen yogurt or fat-free ice cream on the side.*

non-stick cooking spray
1 3/4 cups all-purpose flour
1/2 teaspoon baking soda
1/2 teaspoon ground ginger
1/4 teaspoon ground cloves
1 teaspoon ground cinnamon

1/2 cup sugar
1/4 cup corn syrup
1/4 cup dark molasses
3 egg whites, whipped with a fork
2 tablespoons vegetable oil
1/2 cup apple juice

Preheat oven to 325° F. Spray an 8-inch baking pan with non-stick cooking spray.

In a large bowl, mix flour, baking soda and spices. In a smaller bowl, use an electric mixer to blend sugar, corn syrup, molasses, egg whites, oil and apple juice. Mix wet ingredients into dry ingredients and blend well. Pour into prepared pan and bake 30 to 35 minutes. To serve, cut into 16 squares.

To make gingerbread men, eliminate apple juice and 1 egg white. Blend dough by hand adding a little flour so that the dough can be worked. Roll out dough and shape with cookie cutters. Bake 8 to 10 minutes at 350° F. Decorate with sugar-milk icing, if desired. (see page30)

SERVES: 16 ═══ **NUTRITIONAL INFORMATION PER SERVING** ═══

Calories	105	Total Fat	0 g	Cholesterol	0 mg
Calories from Fat	0%	Saturated Fat	0 g	Sodium	45 mg

CARROT COOKIES

These cookies are rich with flavor on their own but if you want to add icing, try the frosting recipe on page 28 (Carrot Cake) or the sugar-milk icing recipe on page 30 (Triple Ripple Cake).

non-stick cooking spray
1/2 cup sugar
1/2 cup corn syrup
2 tablespoons light margarine
4 egg whites
1 3/4 cups all-purpose flour

1 teaspoon baking powder
1 teaspoon cinnamon
1 cup peeled carrots, shredded coarsely
1/2 cup raisins, plumped by steaming
    over boiling water for 5 minutes

Preheat oven to 350° F. Spray a cookie sheet with non-stick cooking spray. In a large bowl, blend sugar, corn syrup, margarine and egg whites. In a medium-sized bowl, combine flour, baking powder and cinnamon. Blend dry ingredients into wet ingredients. Carefully fold in carrots and plumped raisins. Blend well. Drop onto prepared sheet by rounded teaspoonfuls. Recipe makes 36 cookies.

Bake 12 to 15 minutes or until nicely browned. Cool and apply icing, if desired.

1 PER SERVING		NUTRITIONAL INFORMATION PER SERVING*			
Calories	61	Total Fat	1 g	Cholesterol	0 mg
Calories from Fat	6%	Saturated Fat	< 1 g	Sodium	29 mg

* Nutritional information is based on recipe made without Icing.

COOKIE POPS

Children love making and decorating these cookies.

non-stick cooking spray
1/4 cup light margarine
1/4 cup corn syrup
1/2 cup sugar
4 egg whites
1/4 cup nonfat sour cream
1 teaspoon vanilla extract

2 cups all-purpose flour
1/2 teaspoon baking powder
1/4 teaspoon baking soda
30 craft or candy sticks
assorted decorations for cookies: red
   cinnamon candy, dried fruit, corn
   flakes, jelly beans

Preheat oven to 375° F. Spray 2 cookie sheets with non-stick cooking spray.

In a large bowl, blend margarine, corn syrup, sugar, egg whites, sour cream and vanilla extract. In a medium-sized bowl, combine flour, baking powder and baking soda. Mix dry ingredients with wet ingredients to make a workable dough.

Roll into 30 walnut-sized balls and place, well-spaced, on cookie sheets. Insert craft or candy sticks halfway into each ball. Use the bottom of a glass to flatten each ball. (Sprinkling glass bottom with sugar will prevent it from sticking to the dough.)

Use assorted decorations to create faces and patterns on cookies. Bake 12 to 14 minutes or until lightly browned.

1 PER SERVING ═══════ **NUTRITIONAL INFORMATION PER SERVING** ═══════

Calories	58	Total Fat	1 g	Cholesterol	1 mg
Calories from Fat	12%	Saturated Fat	< 1 g	Sodium	36 mg

CHOCOLATE FUDGE CUPCAKES

Cupcakes are always a big hit with kids. This recipe yields 12 full-size cupcakes but if you want to create smaller portions, try making 24 mini-cupcakes.

12 foil baking cups	6 egg whites
1/2 cup cocoa	1 cup sugar
1 cup cake flour, sifted	1 cup nonfat milk
1 teaspoon baking soda	1 teaspoon vanilla extract
1 teaspoon baking powder	1 teaspoon nonfat chocolate syrup

Preheat oven to 350° F. Line 12 muffin tins with baking cups.

In a large bowl, combine cocoa, flour, baking soda and baking powder.

In a separate bowl, use an electric mixer to whip egg whites until frothy. Add sugar, milk, vanilla extract and chocolate syrup. Whip until well-blended. Fold wet ingredients into dry ingredients. Pour batter into baking cups, distributing it evenly. Bake 12 to 15 minutes for full-size cupcakes or 8 to 10 minutes for mini-cupcakes.

SERVES: 12 ═══════ **NUTRITIONAL INFORMATION PER SERVING** ═══════

Calories	54	Total Fat	< 1 g	Cholesterol	0 mg
Calories from Fat	9%	Saturated Fat	0 g	Sodium	135 mg

STRAWBERRY CUPCAKES

Moist and tender cupcakes with fresh strawberries right in the batter.

non-stick cooking spray
1 teaspoon baking powder
1/2 cup 1% buttermilk
2 egg whites
1 1/4 cups all-purpose flour
3/4 cup sugar

1/4 teaspoon salt
2 tablespoons vegetable oil
1/4 cup corn syrup
1 cup fresh strawberries, hulled and
    chopped

Preheat oven to 350° F. Spray 8 muffin tins with non-stick cooking spray.

In a small bowl, blend baking powder with buttermilk and set aside.

In a separate bowl, beat egg whites with an electric mixer until frothy. In a large bowl, mix flour, sugar and salt until well combined. Blend oil and corn syrup into the flour mixture. Add buttermilk mixture and egg whites, beating until very smooth, about 3 minutes. Fold in strawberries. Divide into prepared muffin tins and bake 15 minutes.

SERVES: 8 **NUTRITIONAL INFORMATION PER SERVING**

Calories	215	Total Fat	4 g	Cholesterol	1 mg
Calories from Fat	16%	Saturated Fat	0 g	Sodium	146 mg

HAPPY FACE LEMON PIE

Children love decorating this sherbet pie.

8 ounces crushed graham crackers
2 tablespoons light margarine, melted
1/4 cup corn syrup

1 pint nonfat lemon sherbet
1 4-ounce container nonfat whipped
　　dessert topping

Preheat oven to 350° F. Allow sherbet and topping to thaw.

Make pie crust in a medium-sized bowl, blending graham crackers, margarine and corn syrup. Press onto the bottom and sides of a 9-inch pie pan and bake 10 minutes. Cool.

Scoop sherbet into the cooled pie crust. Decorate with frozen whipped topping, making eyes, nose, mouth, and hair. Place in the freezer for 6 hours or over night. Before cutting, allow to thaw slightly.

Variations
　Use any flavor sherbet or nonfat frozen yogurt.

SERVES: 8	NUTRITIONAL INFORMATION PER SERVING				
Calories	227	Total Fat	4 g	Cholesterol	4 mg
Calories from Fat	17%	Saturated Fat	1 g	Sodium	202 mg

ICE CREAM IN A BAG

Kids are amazed by this trick. You can make your own ice cream at home or on the run. Try packing a cooler with these ingredients and making ice cream on day-trips.

1 cup nonfat milk

2 tablespoons sugar

1/4 teaspoon vanilla extract

2 cups ice

4 tablespoons salt

1 small locking plastic bag

1 medium-sized locking plastic bag

Blend milk, sugar and vanilla extract and seal into the small bag.

When ready to make the ice cream, put ice and salt into the larger bag. Place the small bag inside the larger one. Seal the larger bag. Knead mixture for 5 to 10 minutes or until the ice cream becomes hard. Wipe any salt off the outside of the small ice cream bag, open and eat.

SERVES: 1 ═══════ **NUTRITIONAL INFORMATION PER SERVING** ═══════

Calories	176	Total Fat	0 g	Cholesterol	4 mg
Calories from Fat	2%	Saturated Fat	0 g	Sodium	126 mg

ICE CREAM SANDWICHES

Scrumptious, refreshing and easy to make.

4 large graham crackers

1/2 cup nonfat frozen yogurt or
  fat-free ice cream, vanilla

1 tablespoon nonfat chocolate sauce

Break graham crackers in two. Spread frozen yogurt on half of the pieces. Squirt chocolate sauce onto frozen yogurt. Cover with remaining cracker halves to make sandwiches. Place on a tray and freeze until ready to eat. Makes 4 sandwiches.

1 PER SERVING ═══════ **NUTRITIONAL INFORMATION PER SERVING** ═══════

Calories	69	Total Fat	1 g	Cholesterol	0 mg
Calories from Fat	17%	Saturated Fat	0 g	Sodium	81 mg

HEAVENLY HASH

🕐 *Frosty, creamy and filled with fruit.*

8 paper baking cups
1 16-ounce can fruit cocktail, drained
1/2 cup tiny marshmallows
1 cup nonfat vanilla yogurt

4 tablespoons strawberry fruit spread or
  preserves
fresh strawberry slices

Place baking cups in muffin tin. In a medium bowl, mix fruit cocktail, marshmallows, yogurt, and fruit spread or preserves. Using an ice cream scoop, divide mixture into baking cups. Freeze until firm, about 2 hours. To serve, on a small plate, arrange a few fresh strawberries around Heavenly Hash.

Variation: use Heavenly Hash to top an ice cream cone.

SERVES: 8		NUTRITIONAL INFORMATION PER SERVING			
Calories	172	Total Fat	0 g	Cholesterol	0 mg
Calories from Fat	2%	Saturated Fat	0 g	Sodium	18 mg

CHOCOLATE POPS

As much fun to prepare as they are to eat.

1 cup nonfat milk
2 1/2 tablespoons non-fat
  chocolate syrup

4 3-ounce paper cups
4 craft or candy sticks

Stir chocolate syrup into milk and pour into paper cups. Freeze until slushy. Stand a craft or candy stick into each chocolate pop and freeze until firm, about 4 hours. Briefly rinse cups under warm water before sliding them off of Chocolate Pops.

SERVES: 4		NUTRITIONAL INFORMATION PER SERVING			
Calories	125	Total Fat	1 g	Cholesterol	0 mg
Calories from Fat	3%	Saturated Fat	< 1 g	Sodium	56 mg

CRISP RICE TREAT & VARIATIONS

The following recipes are delicious adaptations of the traditional cereal treat. Fat content has been reduced to one gram or less per serving.

3 cups tiny marshmallows
2 tablespoons light margarine
1/2 teaspoon vanilla extract

5 cups Rice Krispies™ or similar cereal
1 cup gumdrops, cut into snippets

Make a foil lining for a 13 x 9 x 3-inch baking pan. This will help you remove the crisp rice treats.

Put marshmallows and margarine in a large sauce pan. Turn heat on low, and stir constantly until mixture has melted. Add vanilla extract. Mix in cereal and gumdrops, stirring to coat. Remove from heat. Quickly press mixture into prepared pan with wet hands or the back of a spatula. Allow mixture to cool. Invert pan, remove foil and cut into 24 squares.

Variations: add 1/4 cup cocoa to marshmallow mixture.
Calories 123; calories from fat 4%; total fat 1 g; saturated fat 0 g; cholesterol 0 mg; sodium 93 mg

Or add 1/4 cup reduced fat peanut butter to marshmallow mixture.
Calories 132; calories from fat 10%; total fat 1 g; saturated fat 0 g; cholesterol 0 g; sodium 102 mg

SERVES: 24 ══════════ NUTRITIONAL INFORMATION PER SERVING ══════════

Calories	121	Total Fat	< 1 g	Cholesterol	0 mg
Calories from Fat	3%	Saturated Fat	0 g	Sodium	92 mg

GRAHAM SANDWICHES I

Turn graham crackers into special treats.

1 cup confectioners sugar
2 tablespoons fruit juice (orange, apple, or pineapple)

8 large graham crackers

Mix sugar with fruit juice, creating an icing. Break graham crackers in two and spread icing on half of the pieces. Cover with remaining cracker halves to make sandwiches. Makes 8 sandwiches.

1 PER SERVING		NUTRITIONAL INFORMATION PER SERVING			
Calories	105	Total Fat	1 g	Cholesterol	0 mg
Calories from Fat	1%	Saturated Fat	0 g	Sodium	66 mg

GRAHAM SANDWICHES II

8 large graham crackers
1/4 cup reduced-fat, smooth peanut butter

2 bananas, sliced

Break graham crackers in two and spread peanut butter on half of the pieces, 1 1/2 teaspoons per piece. Top with sliced bananas and cover with remaining cracker halves to make sandwiches.

Makes 8 sandwiches.

1 PER SERVING		NUTRITIONAL INFORMATION PER SERVING			
Calories	91	Total Fat	2 g	Cholesterol	0 mg
Calories from Fat	19%	Saturated Fat	< 1 g	Sodium	74 mg

TRAIL MIX

Often eaten by hikers for a quick energy boost, trail mix makes a great lunch-box addition for the kids.

1/2 cup raisins
1/4 cup dried apricot
1/2 cup dried banana chips

1/4 dry-roasted peanuts
1/2 cup nonfat granola

Mix all ingredients. Store in an air-tight container.

SERVES: 6		NUTRITIONAL INFORMATION PER SERVING			
Calories	120	Total Fat	2 g	Cholesterol	0 mg
Calories from Fat	11%	Saturated Fat	0 g	Sodium	109 mg

MERINGUE KISSES

Light, sweet treats that are easy to make.

12 x 16-inch piece brown paper
  (a paper bag works fine)
6 egg whites, at room temperature

1/2 teaspoon cream of tartar
1/3 cup sugar

Preheat oven to 200° F. Place brown paper on a baking sheet. Whip egg whites with an electric mixer. Blend in cream of tartar. When egg whites are frothy, sprinkle sugar, a teaspoon at a time, over egg whites. Continue beating egg whites until stiff and sugar is incorporated well. (You can tell this by pinching a bit of the whipped egg white between your fingers. If sugar has been incorporated, you will feel no grains.) Drop by spoonfuls onto paper making little peaks or kisses. (These kisses can also be formed by filling a pastry bag with the batter and squeezing kisses onto the baking sheet.) Bake for 2 hours. Makes 24 kisses.

1 PER SERVING		NUTRITIONAL INFORMATION PER SERVING			
Calories	14	Total Fat	0 g	Cholesterol	0 mg
Calories from Fat	0%	Saturated Fat	0 g	Sodium	13 mg

POPCORN BALLS

These popcorn balls are fun and easy to make. Just rinse your hands in cold water before shaping balls.

3/4 cup sugar

3 tablespoons light margarine

1/3 cup corn syrup

1/2 teaspoon vanilla extract

8 cups air-popped popcorn

In a small sauce pan, combine sugar, margarine and corn syrup. Heat to boiling and stir constantly for 5 minutes. Remove from heat and stir in vanilla extract. Place popcorn in a large bowl. Pour syrup over it and toss with fork to blend. Wash hands and rinse with cold water. When popcorn mixture has cooled slightly, form into 8 balls. Store in plastic wrap.

SERVES: 8		NUTRITIONAL INFORMATION PER SERVING			
Calories	168	Total Fat	2 g	Cholesterol	< 1 mg
Calories from Fat	11%	Saturated Fat	< 1 g	Sodium	105 mg

CARAMEL CORN

This terrific low-fat recipe was adapted from the 1982 edition of the WFIN (Findlay, Ohio) Phone Club Cook Book.

1/2 cup brown sugar, packed

2 tablespoons light margarine

1/4 cup corn syrup (dark or light)

1/8 teaspoon baking soda

dash salt

2 quarts air-popped popcorn

Preheat oven to 200° F. Bring brown sugar, margarine and corn syrup to a boil in a heavy sauce pan. Reduce heat and simmer for 4 minutes. Remove from heat. Add soda and salt. Stir well. Place popcorn in a large, shallow pan and pour caramel sauce over it. Stir to coat well. Bake for 1 hour, stirring several times. Remove and cool. Break into 8 servings.

SERVES: 8		NUTRITIONAL INFORMATION PER SERVING			
Calories	220	Total Fat	< 1 g	Cholesterol	0 mg
Calories from Fat	6%	Saturated Fat	< 1 g	Sodium	211 mg

APPLE CRISP

🕐 *Nonfat vanilla frozen yogurt is a delicious complement to warm apple crisps.*

non-stick cooking spray
1/2 cup cereal (such as corn flakes or
  crisp rice cereal)
1 teaspoon cinnamon
1 teaspoon light margarine

1 tablespoon corn syrup
2 large apples, peeled and sliced
1 teaspoon fresh lime juice
1/4 cup sugar

Preheat oven to 400° F. Spray a 4-cup baking pan with non-stick cooking spray.

In a medium-sized bowl, blend cereal, cinnamon, margarine and corn syrup. In a separate bowl, combine apples, lime juice and sugar. Pour apple mixture into baking pan and top with cereal mixture. Bake 25 to 30 minutes or until cereal is crisp and lightly browned.

SERVES: 4		NUTRITIONAL INFORMATION PER SERVING			
Calories	119	Total Fat	< 1 g	Cholesterol	0 mg
Calories from Fat	5%	Saturated Fat	< 1 g	Sodium	59 mg

CINNAMON CRISPS

Keep a shaker full of cinnamon sugar to make Cinnamon Crisps at a moment's notice.

1 6-inch flour tortilla
1 teaspoon sugar

1/4 teaspoon cinnamon

Preheat oven to 450° F. Place tortilla flat on a baking pan. Sprinkle with sugar and cinnamon. Bake 5 minutes or until sugar starts to caramelize. Cut into wedges and serve.

SERVES: 1		NUTRITIONAL INFORMATION PER SERVING			
Calories	110	Total Fat	< 1 g	Cholesterol	< 1 mg
Calories from Fat	15%	Saturated Fat	< 1 g	Sodium	< 1 mg

GELATIN JIGGLES

When preparing gelatin, the possibilities are endless. Try pouring the gelatin into candy molds for a variety of shapes. For a rainbow effect, layer different flavors of gelatin, allowing each to gel for at least an hour before adding next layer.

2 6-ounce packages gelatin
   dessert, flavored

2 1/2 cups apple juice

Place gelatin powder in a large bowl. Instead of water, use apple juice to make gelatin. Heat apple juice to boiling and pour over gelatin powder. Pour into a 13 x 9-inch pan. Refrigerate at least 3 hours. Cut into squares or triangles or cut into other shapes with cookie cutters.

SERVES: 24 ══════ **NUTRITIONAL INFORMATION PER SERVING** ══════

Calories	59	Total Fat	0 g	Cholesterol	0 mg
Calories from Fat	0%	Saturated Fat	0 g	Sodium	7 mg

BLACK COW

A nonfat rootbeer float is a special treat for any occasion.

1 scoop (1/2 cup) nonfat frozen yogurt
   or fat-free ice cream, vanilla

1/2 cup root beer
1/2 cup club soda

Scoop the frozen yogurt into a large, 12-ounce glass. Pour root beer over the yogurt and bring to a fizz with club soda.

Variations: make a white cow by substituting ginger ale for root beer. Make a purple cow by substituting grape juice.

SERVES: 1 ══════ **NUTRITIONAL INFORMATION PER SERVING*** ══════

Calories	51	Total Fat	0 g	Cholesterol	0 mg
Calories from Fat	0%	Saturated Fat	0 g	Sodium	51 mg

* Nutritional information for variations is the same as for the original.

TROPICAL BANANA SMOOTHIE

Smoothies have all the froth and flavor of a milk shake without all the fat.

1/2 cup freshly squeezed orange juice
  with pulp
1/2 cup papaya juice (or half the meat
  of a papaya or mango)

1 ripe banana
1 cup ice cubes

Place all ingredients into a blender. Blend on the highest speed until smooth, about 3 minutes.

SERVES: 2		NUTRITIONAL INFORMATION PER SERVING			
Calories	117	Total Fat	1 g	Cholesterol	0 mg
Calories from Fat	5%	Saturated Fat	< 1 g	Sodium	2 mg

FRUIT FREEZE FIZZIE

Serve as a summer dessert or as a daytime snack.

1 6-ounce can frozen pineapple
  concentrate
1 6-ounce can frozen orange juice
  concentrate

1 tablespoon honey
1 medium banana
1-liter bottle club soda
2-liter bottle lemon-lime soda

Allow pineapple and orange juice concentrates to thaw. Pour them into a blender with honey and banana. Blend until smooth. Pour into a 9-inch loaf pan and freeze until solid, about 6 hours. To serve, scoop 1/4 cup frozen mixture into a 12-ounce glass. Add a little club soda and fill remainder of glass with lemon lime soda. Stir.

SERVES: 8		NUTRITIONAL INFORMATION PER SERVING			
Calories	177	Total Fat	0 g	Cholesterol	0 mg
Calories from Fat	0%	Saturated Fat	0 g	Sodium	30 mg

INDEX